PROFITING
PH**BY**ONE

No Nonsense Skills and Techniques for
Selling and Getting Leads by Telephone

JIM DOMANSKI

D1445620

Business By Phone Inc.™
13254 Stevens, Omaha, NE 68137
www.businessbyphone.com

Profiting By Phone--No Nonsense Skills and Techniques for Selling and Getting Leads By Telephone
By Jim Domanski

Copyright 2004, Business By Phone Inc.

Published By:
Business By Phone Inc.
13254 Stevens St.
Omaha, NE 68137.
(402)895-9399
Fax:(402)896-3353
E-mail ArtS@BusinessByPhone.com
http://www.BusinessByPhone.com

Author: Jim Domanski
Jim Domanski
613-591-1998
http://www.teleconceptsconsulting.com

Cover design by George Foster, Foster & Foster, Fairfield, IA

ISBN 1-881081-08-7

Dedication

To my mom and dad for providing me with all the "right stuff."

To my sons, Kevin and Craig, for the continuous joy and inspiration.

And finally to wife, Bev, for "putting up with all the hassles."

Special Thanks . . .

A special thanks to Art Sobczak: an inspiration, a mentor, a guide, a friend ... and a jouster of wits!

To Tricia Lewandowski, for her keen eye, and always friendly voice!

Contents

Contents

Foreword

By Art Sobczak, President, Business By Phone Inc.

People sometimes ask why I have a person who is somewhat in competition with the training side of my business write a column for my newsletter, ***Telephone Selling Report***. I guess they'll especially be perplexed now that I've published his book.

My reasoning? Jim Domanski is good. Period.

You see, my mission . . . my entire business existence . . . is based upon providing professionals with proven telesales ideas to get more business. No one has the exclusive on good ideas, and when I see something that is solid, fresh, and presented in a way that people can use instantly, I owe it to my market to provide it to them. To you. And Jim does that. He has been doing it for over seven years in my newsletter, and I'm proud to provide these profitable ideas and strategies to you in this book.

Jim and I have similar sales philosophies. So similar, in fact, that our frequent telephone calls, faxes, and e-mails turn into good-natured ribbing about who stole what ideas from whom. You'll see in this book that Jim isn't of the hard-sell ilk (very few Canadians are, which everyone can learn a lesson from). We both believe that the only professional way to sell is to help someone buy.

And what I particularly like about Jim's style is that he has the uncommon ability to take an idea, theory, or process, simplify it for those of us who care more about the real world how-to than the why, and bring it to life with entertaining examples and stories . . . things we experience every day in the trenches.

And when I read a book or a attend a seminar, I want to be certain I'm getting instruction from someone who isn't just regurgitating material they read or heard elsewhere. Rather, I want stuff from someone who's actually done it. If that appeals to you, too, Jim is your guy. He has been there and done that. He has lived this stuff, suffered the beatings of the school of telesales hard knocks like most of us, and is able to share his observations and teachings in his uniquely entertaining style.

If you are serious about your success—and I would wager that you are because you're reading the *Foreword* of a how-to book, for gosh sakes—I am confident you will show noticeable results in your sales and attitude within days, and certainly within weeks of reading this book.

I admire your ambition and desire, and congratulate you in advance on the success you'll show as a result of using the ideas you're about to read.

Here's to your continued success!

Introduction

When I conduct telesales training seminars I begin the session by giving all the attendees a little test. Try it now.

Start by crossing your arms. Look down. Your right arm is over your left or your left is over your right. Whatever it is, switch it.

How does it feel?

If you are like most people, the comments usually include things like "It feels uncomfortable," "different," "strange," "awkward" or "unusual."

I explain that the point of the exercise is to demonstrate that when we implement "change," there is bound to be a certain level of discomfort and awkwardness. In sales we get used to certain skills and techniques. They become habits. And even though they may not be the best skills or techniques, and even though they may not be very effective, we use them simply because they "feel" good. We become comfortable with them. And even if there is something new out there that might help improve our efforts, we tend to resist them.

I tell the attendees that the skills and techniques they are about to learn might make them feel a little uncomfortable and awkward. But just as they were capable of crossing their arms with some thought, so too are they capable of implementing these ideas with some thought.

Many of the ideas and suggestions in this book will make you feel uncomfortable because they are new, or different from what you are used to. If you feel uncomfortable that's good. It means you are stretching and learning.

Virtually every technique and method listed in the book is based on real life selling and lead generation situations. I wish I could say that I created everyone of these successful ideas. I can't. I can say that since 1981 I have amalgamated literally hundreds of ideas and tips from telesales and field reps across North America. What you are about to read are their ideas. Ideas that have worked. They are proven.

The challenge for you is to try them. Change is difficult for most of us. You will hesitate. You will rationalize and say "It's not my way of selling," or "It won't work in my situation."

Bull.

For the most part, the ideas listed here have worked in dozens of industries with hundreds of clients. Try them. Try them honestly. Practice them and then try them and watch what happens.

The 1% Solution

One last thought. I call it the "1% Solution."

While there might be a few ideas in the book that can bring *dramatic* improvement in your results (such as the "Humble Approach to Opening Statements"), for the most part the ideas are cumulative in their effect. My objective is not to improve your skill level by 100% in any one given area. The objective is to improve your skill level 1% or 2 % in a **hundred** different areas. This cumulative affect will make you more effective, more well-rounded, and much more successful in sales.

About Jim Domanski and Teleconcepts Consulting

I started Teleconcepts Consulting back in 1992 after spending about ten years with Bell Canada. In the very early 1980's I worked with Bell as a field representative selling telephone systems. One day I visited a prospect with the objective of closing a sale. To my surprise and utter amazement he explained he had just purchased a telephone system . . . over the telephone from a company about 150 miles away!

While somewhat disappointed, I was intrigued by the implication. Selling telephone systems was always the realm of field sales. The mold was broken. I was so intrigued that I pounced on the opportunity to join a consulting division within the phone company called Phone Power. Phone Power's mandate was to increase long distance revenues by consulting with companies on how to use the telephone more strategically as a sales and marketing tool.

The concept of using the phone more effectively in these two disciplines was still relatively new. But it boomed. I had found my niche in life.

I shouldn't have been surprised. In an earlier job as a sales rep with a firm out of Atlanta, I learned the power of the telephone. Instead of racing across my territory I sat, phone in ear, learning about lead generation. The good and the bad. The good being what it could do for me in terms of having a qualified lead. The bad in that I made about 600 mistakes as I learned how to craft messages, scripts, and follow-ups. Tremendous experience.

But selling a $6000 phone system was something else. I knew I had to check it out.

For about six years I helped implement telephone selling and lead generation programs. I did the "soup to nuts" kind of thing. I helped recruit and hire telephone sales reps; created motivation and incentive programs; drafted, and redrafted scripts and call guides; trained both inbound and outbound reps on how to sell and service by phone; worked with others in developing tracking systems; monitored calls; coached and coached and coached; wrote ad copy for lead generation letters . . . you name it, I did it.

In 1989 I had an opportunity to write about telemarketing in Canada. This allowed me to travel across Canada and interview companies who had implemented unique and successful telephone selling and customer service programs. It was a wonderful and enlightening experience. Whereas I had spent so much time in the trenches actually doing and implementing the telephone programs, this project gave me the opportunity to see the "big picture." In other words, how telephone sales could be implemented into the company's strategic plan. How it could make a difference. I loved it.

Cocky guy that I was I decided to leave the "security" of the telephone company and start my own consulting firm. And it has been great.

Teleconcepts provides two key services. The first is consulting for outbound telephone sales and lead generation programs. I help companies strategically plan and then implement start-up telephone selling and lead generation programs. Teleconcepts also provides an "audit and review" consulting process for firms with existing outbound call centers. The objective here, of course, is to analyze the center and look for opportunities to improve productivity, performance and profitability.

The second service provided by Teleconcepts is my first love: Training.

Training is what makes the call center successful. You can have the best planned call center staffed with great personnel and supported by all sorts of marketing material, but it the reps can't communicate and sell effectively, it won't work.

Outbound selling and lead generation is a unique kind of beast. In the absence of face-to-face contact, selling and marketing by telephone is challenging at the best of times. Teleconcepts provides both generic and customized training ranging from one to four days in length depending on your requirements.

Believing that training is an ongoing activity, I am in the process of developing a newsletter that bridges strategy and applications with skills and techniques. Targeted for supervisors and managers this newsletter is a much-needed educational tool in the outbound call center "industry."

If you would like any additional information on the consulting or training (or anything else for that matter) please give me call, fax me, e-mail or write me.

In the meantime, continued success!

Jim Domanski
Kanata, Ontario
(613)591-1998
fax: (613)591-1707
e-mail: jim.domanski@sympatico.ca

Section One
Pre-Call
Planning

2

How to Get Better Results By Using a Script

Just suppose there was a way to shorten your call and improve your overall communication impact with your prospects and customers. This would likely mean you could make more calls in less time, which really means you would meet and exceed your sales objectives—faster. Ultimately, if you're paid on commission, it would mean better earning potential.

Well, there is a way. It's called a script.

Given a choice, most sales reps would rather pull teeth from their lower gum with pliers than use a script. But, like it or not, well-crafted scripts work. And they work well.

Throughout the book I'll make reference to scripts; how to develop them, and how to use them in the sales process.

What? Everyone Resists Using Scripts

Typically, sales reps resist scripts because they're "canned," lack personality and spontaneity, and don't allow for natural conversational interaction between the rep and the prospect/customer. (You could probably add more reasons, and I'd be inclined to agree with you in every case.)

But before you start wrenching away with those pliers, let's define "script." Most say it's "a word-for-word presentation from start to finish." My definition is a little different. I maintain it's a word-for-word presentation—in certain key parts.

Smart managers, supervisors, and sales reps recognize that

a good sales presentation can't be totally scripted because the customer or prospect rarely adheres to what you've written. And unless you're selling a basic commodity like carpet cleaning it is difficult to script for the vast majority of sales calls.

Yet, some parts should be scripted. Certain segments of your presentation, that, when scripted, make the call progress smoothly while reducing call length.

The opening of every call should be scripted. I am staggered and amazed when I see reps make up a new opening line thirty, forty, even fifty times daily. It doesn't make sense. The opening statement is the key to success. Once you have found the right mix of words (the magic key) don't mess with it.

In general, product descriptions should be scripted as well. While some customization is expected—especially benefits— the product more or less remains constant with all customers. Why reinvent the wheel? Use a job aid such as a feature-advantage-benefit chart.

Objections also come in a variety of flavors and colors, but they, too, can be anticipated. Specific replies can and should be produced. Job aids, again, are remarkably helpful.

Finally, there are certain parts of the closing remarks that can be scripted; repeating the key details of the agreement, sale, or other action items is not only courteous, but it avoids some nasty misunderstandings down the line.

Whether you realize it or not, you are probably using scripts—or parts of them—in your dialogue right now. Beginning with the next chapter, and elsewhere through this book, I'll show you ways to make that dialogue more powerful, getting you more results. Read with an open mind, and you might be surprised what you'll learn.

3

Script Preparation: What to Do Before Writing

Scripting begins with grunt work. A little bit of thought before you put pen to paper saves you time and keeps you focused.

Typically, a supervisor or a manager should tackle most of these issues. However, you as a responsible, "proactive" sales rep should ask these same questions. Knowing the answers makes the delivery of the script easier and makes you more successful. Here are questions you should ask yourself.

1. What is the overall goal?

What is it you are trying to do? Do you want to sell, qualify, make an appointment, educate, or build a relationship? The answer to the question will dictate everything from your opening statement through to your closing.

2. Who are you calling?

Are you calling a decision maker, an influencer, a secretary, a purchasing agent? Do you have a specific name? A title, position or department? Sometimes, you might be in contact with any number of these people in a single call or a series of calls. Should you have a series of scripts that prepares you for any of these contacts? Build a profile of each. What makes them "tick"? What's in it for them?

3. What is the product or service you are offering?

Is it complex or simple? Complex products are not usually sold or even qualified on a single call. Often there are a series of calls that move the prospect or customer further down the sales cycle. If you have a product or marketing department, haul them in and pick their brains. Typically, they are the experts, so utilize them.

4. Set objectives.

Objectives differ from goals. Objectives refer to what you want to do in that particular call. For example, you might have as a goal to sell a connection to the Internet. However this usually takes three or four calls. Thus the objective of the call might be to generate interest, qualify and get literature in the hands of the prospect. The objective of the second call might be to get the prospect to focus on specific applications. The objective of the third call might be to sell the connection.

5. What questions should you ask?

Jot these down for every situation. In essence they become a checklist of things that must be asked or the call objective will not be met. Remember, the types of questions asked will vary with each target market. If you are qualifying leads or setting up appointments for field reps, have the rep come in on your scripting session. Let them tell you the types of questions that they need answered.

6. Do you need support material?

For example, do you have literature you can send or material you can fax? Review your existing material. Is it conducive to telephone selling? Should it be revised or revamped for your situation?

7. What strategy or approach to the market do you want?

Do you want to send (or fax or courier) information first and then follow up with a phone call? Or should you call first, qualify and then send? Or perhaps you will not support the call at all.

8. What about fulfillment?

If you promise to send something out or complete an order, when will it be done and who will do it? Many a program lies in mediocrity or disaster because someone did not tell the inventory people or fulfillment house that a new program was beginning.

These questions will likely generate more questions. And that is good. The secret to good scripting is good preparation.

4

18 Reasons Customers Say "Yes"

Being a Canadian, recalling the awesome victories of the Toronto Blue Jays a few years ago always leaves me with a positive mental attitude. I'm in one of those euphoric moods as I'm writing this, so I thought it appropriate to examine the more positive side of selling.

Most writers will spend a great deal of time telling you why prospects and customers say no. Instead, let's look at why customers say "yes."(The following list is a condensed version of those described by William Davis in his book, *"The Salesman's Handbook."*)

Customers/Prospects Say "Yes" Because . . .

1. They actually want what you have to offer.

2. They feel it will benefit their company.

3. Some fear if they do not buy it now, they will have to pay more later.

4. Some customers can't resist anything new.

5. Believe it or not, there are those who like to spend money.

6. They like you, your style and your professionalism.

7. They are not happy with their present supplier or salesperson.

8. Time. Some customers are in a hurry and want to save time.

9. They think it will make them look good. It's an ego thing.

10. They want to take advantage of a discount or special offer.

11. They like making gutsy or bold decisions.

12. The competition uses your product or service and has done well with it.

13. They lack the courage to say "no."

14. Some are, quite frankly, greedy.

15. They feel insecure.

16. They actually *need* your product (which differs from merely wanting it.)

17. You catch them in the right mood.

18. They are afraid someone else will beat them to it.

The key point to these factors is that there is a positive side to selling. I think a good many sales reps dwell too much on why people say no, that they condition themselves into believing that every sale is a chore. They build or create needless stress. This leads to discouragement and burnout.

Try posting this list on your desk and read them through prior to making your calls. Condition yourself to the positive side of selling.

5

Dealing With Difficult Names: Yours and Theirs

What do you do when you have one of those unpronounceable names like Wciezjeikie, or worse, Sobczak? I have actually met sales reps who become annoyed to the point of being indignant when a prospect or customer stumbles over their name.

When Your Name is Unique

The first option is simple: Change your name! Not legally, of course, but for the sake of making the call easier. Now for those of you who have ethnic pride, like myself, don't get upset. You must remember that you are calling a customer. The operative word is "customer."

You should make the call as easy as possible for him or her. Think of yourself as an actor or actress with a stage name. If your name is a roadblock, remove it. It is only a temporary thing, and it will relieve you of a lot of stress. And, incidentally, it will relieve the customer's stress. Many of them are well aware that saying your name is a difficult chore, and that mispronouncing it is an embarrassment to them. (By the way, if you do change your name, select something that is unusual but not bizarre. It makes you unique, and generally, the customer will remember it better than the standard fare.)

Warren Blanding, Chairman of the Customer Service Institute, wrote me about a rep whose name is Donna Przybylkiewicz. She says her name is one of her strongest assets. Customers at first can't believe it is her real name, but they never forget it after she pronounces it. Warren explained that Donna feels her name is an excellent icebreaker and talking point. What's more, Donna uses her name to get a couple of chuckles. She tells customers and prospects that Przybylkiewicz is her married name; her maiden name was Donna Smith!

The point is well taken. Rather then seeing her name as a possible obstacle in her calling Donna chooses to see it as a key selling ingredient.

In selling there will always be obstacles to overcome. Try using a different mindset when you encounter a difficult situation. Consider flipping the issue. See if you can make the obstacle a benefit.

Contrary to popular belief, changing your name will not change your identity or personality. It is not the name that counts, but what's inside!

When Their Name is Unique

And, what do you do when the customer has an unpronounceable name? Good question. Before picking up the phone, try pronouncing it. Ask others around you. Scribble it phonetically. Or, if he or she has an easy first name, you might want to try using that instead of the surname.

> **Tip:** Call the company's operator, or the prospect's secretary or receptionist. Ask for the pronunciation. Or, call at off hours and you might just get voice mail (here's a time when you're hoping for it!) Listen carefully for the pronunciation.

Suppose you're still stuck, the first name is unavailable and you are stuck with a surname with 18 letters and no vowels? Well, try saying it, and then ask the customer if you did indeed pronounce it correctly. Be ready with pen in hand at this point. Listen closely to the pronunciation and then phonetically write the name down. For example, Opincariu would be "o-pen-care-eeyu." Repeat it slowly back to the customer and ask if you have it correctly.

Don't be afraid to ask the origin of the name. Names are

interesting. The first two examples provided above are Polish, the second, Opincariu, is Romanian. After a while you will appreciate the manner in which you have tackled the name. Believe me, they have experienced every manner of mispronunciation and will likely be impressed that you made an honest attempt to tackle it.

Of course, if you cannot wrap your mouth around the word, you might want to ignore its use completely. Sometimes that gets awkward. Instead, you might want to get a little old fashioned and use "sir" or "madam."

If You Have Something In Common . . .

Sales rep, Rocky Mancini, tells me that when he recognizes an Italian name, he speaks a little Italian to the prospect. Sometimes it breaks the ice and establishes a common bond, especially those who are fluent in Italian. Even those who do not speak Italian acknowledge his effort. He has never encountered negative effects.

The topic of names and ethnic origins is an issue of importance. Pay heed and take care the next time you encounter a twelve-syllable name.

6

Use Stage Directions With Your Presentation

Visiting a telesales center in Prince Edward Island, I became nosy and leafed through the training material developed by the supervisor, Peggy. I stumbled across a script that was triple spaced and beneath it, written in red, were "delivery tips." Here is a brief excerpt from the portion dealing with objections.

> **Customer:** "The price is too high."
>
> **Sales Rep:** *"Hmmm...that's an interesting point. Just suppose a moment . . .* (pause) *. . . Hmm* (ruminating . . . slow, contemplative tone . . . pause)"

I asked Peggy about the notes and she explained that she did some part-time acting and that when learning a script the actors and actresses would often make notes to give their script character. Initially the notes served as prompts until the script delivery was mastered.

When training her telephone reps, Peggy incorporated the same technique when it came to role playing. She explained that the first few role plays are always awkward and this technique helped make the process easier. Good idea.

But Peggy also explained that their center will run various outbound programs for a number of products at different times of the year. Each product has a different script that can often be resurrected and the script notes help get the sales rep into the groove faster.

Moreover, she explained that like any telesales operation,

there was a certain degree of turnover. This training aid helped move trainees along faster with less effort from Peggy.

It dawned on me again that the best movie and stage actors "read" scripts, but with meaning and character. But, before they earn their Emmy or Oscar they have to put some time and effort into the part. You might want to remember this the next time you are handed a script, or write one of your own. Pause for a moment. Picture yourself as a budding star. Prepare for your part by jotting down notes and reminders of how you should deliver a particular line. And then, practice, practice, practice.

Give it a try and . . . break a leg!

Section Two: Telephone Prospecting

7

How to Cold Call Lists Without Contact Names

O ne of the most difficult chores for a sales rep to perform is to make cold calls from a list without names.
A list without names also implies that you may know little else
about the company. Hence, a doubly difficult task. Here are
some tips on how to make the calling process more effective.

Tips for Profitable Cold Calling

❑ **Build a target profile.** Chances are you have already done
this. But just in case, before calling, determine precisely with
whom it is you wish to speak. Is it a department head, an office
manager, the communications officer?

❑ **Use directory assistance or a phone book.** Find the
general number for the company. Lump this activity into a single
session. In other words, if you have a list of 100 companies, get
the telephone numbers first. Don't call directory assistance,
get the number and immediately make the sales call. The reason is simple enough. You want to have enough numbers to get
you on a roll.

❑ **Call the general number.** Speak to the receptionist, op-
erator, or secretary in order to acquire the name of your target
contact (as defined in your target profile). Here is an example.

> "Good morning. This Is Debbie Taylor calling from
> Eco-System Consulting Services. I was wonder-
> ing if you could help me? (long pause) I am trying
> to determine who would be in charge of market-
> ing the services of your clinic?'

A few points to note: First, identify yourself and your company. People are more apt to be cooperative and give you information when they know who you are.

Second, ensure your tone is respectful and sincere. Sales reps can really blow it here, so watch it. Don't rattle off the words and make it sound like a demand. Few people respond effectively to a demand.

Third, use the long pause after the question. This Is vital. The pause dramatically increases your chances of success because it requires a response. Besides, the chances of someone refusing to help you are slim. Listen to whether or not the receptionist provides his/her name. And then use it:

> **Receptionist:** "Bayshore Animal Clinic. This Is Fiona. How may I help you?"
>
> **Sales Rep:** "Good morning Fiona. This is Debbie Taylor from Eco-System Consulting Service. Fiona (pause) I was wondering if you could help me?" (long pause)

The use of the name is a simple but effective technique. It quickly personalizes the conversation and causes the person to focus entirely on the next several words you utter.

❏ **Be prepared to elaborate.** That's why you have a target market profile. In the example above, the clinic may not have a marketing person and/or the receptionist may have no idea what you are talking about. For example,

> **Sales Rep:** "Let me clarify a bit. I am looking for the person who might be in charge of placing a newspaper ad or in charge of producing flyers that promote your clinic to pet owners."
>
> **Receptionist:** "Oh, that would be Deanna Scott. She is the head technician and office manager."

❏ **Do not have your call transferred . . . at this time.** Some reps might gasp in horror at this suggestion. My recommendation is that you make the hundred calls with the single objective of gathering the names of your targeted prospects. The reasoning is similar to the above: you want to be able to have a pool of names that allow you to continue to call. This allows you to get and stay on a roll. Besides, if the secretary or receptionist was willing to put you through then, it is likely they will do it again in the future.

❏ **Use the opportunity to gather more information.** For example, determining when would be a good time to call back.

❏ **Be sure to thank the person who has helped you out.** You don't have to gush, but some form of appreciation is important: "Thanks Fiona. I really appreciate your help."

❏ **Make friends.** Use the rapport you have established with the secretary/receptionist when you do call back. For example:

> "Oh hi Fiona. It's Debbie Taylor from Eco-System Consulting Services. You helped me out on Tuesday when you gave me Deanna's name. Is she available?"

In this example, you reestablished the fact that Fiona had helped you. In essence, you are saying thank you once again, and in some small measure, you are continuing to build rapport.

❏ **Play the numbers.** Occasionally you will run into an uncooperative receptionist or a company who utilizes voice mail or auto attendants to manage the flow of calls. Here's a tip. Play with variations of the general number in an attempt to reach a live person. For example. if the general telephone number is 592-5200, try dialing 592-5208. Chances are this is a direct dial extension. Continue this until you reach a live voice. Your procedure is much the same.

> "Good morning. This is Debbie Taylor from Eco-System Consulting. I have been trying to get to the person who handles your marketing program but unfortunately I seem to have ended up at your extension. I was wondering if you could help me?"

Most people are acquainted with the frustration of automated voice systems and they are only too glad to assist.

In summary, these tips will help warm up your cold calling. Stay warm!

8

How to Generate Qualified Leads By Phone

Developing a good, qualified lead can be challenging and frustrating. Regardless of whether you're getting leads for inside or outside sales reps, here are some tips on how to make lead generation programs more effective.

1. Involve the field (or inside) sales reps.

This is so important I can't stress it enough. After all, the sales reps are the ones who must respond to the leads. Sales reps are a curious breed of cat, especially field reps. If the leads don't pan out to their expectations they tend to become a bit skittish about the subsequent leads passed on to them. They collectively claim, "That's not how I would qualify a lead."

Create a workshop and have a sales rep or two (or more) join you during your scripting session. Ask them what they consider to be a qualified lead. Ask them about the types of questions they would ask the prospect.

2. Limit the number of questions.

Too few questions can result in a poorly qualified lead. On the other hand, too many questions can turn a prospect off. The objective is to qualify the lead, not to begin the selling process. It is up to the field rep to expand the questioning phase. In most circumstances, you should limit your qualifying to no more than 7-8 key questions. This is about the maximum number a prospect will allow you. Anything more becomes annoying to the prospect and may dilute the quality of the answers.

3. Be up front about your objective.

Let the prospect know what you are about to do:

"Mr. Besta, This is Adrian Molle calling on behalf
of the Retail Merchants Association. The reason
for my call is to follow up on a package we sent
you concerning our business insurance program.
Mr. Besta, I have no way of knowing if our business insurance could benefit you, but if I could
take a couple of minutes and ask you some questions perhaps I could determine if we can save you
money on your insurance or improve your coverage. How does that sound?"

4. Ask the questions.

Usually the qualifiers should be a blend of open- and closed-
ended questions. If, however, you have seven or eight closed
questions be careful that you don't give the impression that
you are interrogating the prospect. To avoid this, break the
questioning sequence up in the middle. For example, after you
have asked three or four questions you might want to say, "Okay,
Mr. Besta, I just have a few more questions and that will be it."

5. Use the "final qualifier."

Here is a question that has dramatically improved the results of a number of lead generation programs,

"Mr. Besta, if we can provide a better premium or
better coverage, is there any reason why we cannot do business?"

The objective of this question is to determine if there is
anything preventing the client from going further into the selling process. It is amazing what you will learn from this question. Little things, like the prospect buys his insurance from
his father, or his broker is his neighbor and friend, or that he
has a special discount agreement. (While I've used an example
from the insurance field, this question can be used in any industry.)

This question, in effect, gives the prospect one last chance
to disqualify himself. And that's okay. You don't want to send
out a rep only to discover there really was no opportunity.

6. Determine if you have a qualified lead or not.

If the prospect is not qualified, say so:

"Mr. Besta, based on what you have told me about

> your business, I do not think I would be able to
> provide you with a competitive quote at this time.
> But I do want to thank you for the time and the
> opportunity."

If the prospect does qualify, explain what happens next.

> "Mr. Besta, it sounds like we might be able to save
> you some money or improve your coverage. I am
> going to have Jack Davidson, our field represen-
> tative, give you a call within the next two days to
> set up an appointment."

Note 1: There is no question asked. Based on the perceived benefit, the rep explains what he or she will do and does not ask permission or consent. (The prospect, of course, might have some sort of objection but these can be anticipated. This has been a very effective way of setting up appointments.)

Note 2: There is a specific time frame of two days for follow up given to the prospect. This is important. Hot leads have a way of cooling off if left uncontacted too long. It is vital that the field reps call within 48 hours to make the initial contact.

7. Follow up on the lead.

Approximately 72 hours after the lead has been initiated, I have reps make a follow up call to the prospect. The objective of the call is to ensure that the field rep has made the initial contact. Am I checking up on the field rep? You bet. And it is amazing how effective the procedure can be in getting the out-side reps to make contact. It's equally startling to see how the leads begin to convert. When following up on the client, you might want to say,

> "Mr. Besta, it's Adrian Molle calling from the Re-
> tail Merchants Association. We spoke a couple of
> days ago. The reason for my call was to see If you
> had a chance to speak with Jack Davidson."

While there is a element of "checking up" involved, there is also the added benefit of demonstrating to the prospect your company's level of commitment and dedication.

9

Qualifying and Disqualifying Sales Prospects

I can't say I have read a lot of stuff by the German philosopher, Goethe, but I do remember one pithy little quote:

"There has been nothing new since the Renaissance."

And I think he's right when it comes to telephone selling.

There is nothing particularly new when it comes to telephone selling, but there are variations on a theme.

For example, the methodology of qualifying a sales prospect probably hasn't changed much since the Renaissance. Here are some tips and ideas that may not necessarily be new but certainly have not lost their value.

Understanding Disqualification

"Go For the No" is a quote that has been around for a while. Essentially the phrase suggests that it is as important to *disqualify* a lead as it is to qualify a lead. In fact, disqualification is a qualifier.

For example, I recently met with a sales rep who proudly proclaimed he had qualified 63 prospects for the month of May. Over the next two months, the rep busily spent his time working on written proposals for each prospect. Sadly, by mid-August he had closed only three of these, while 57 had been rejected, and the remainder were pending. In a company with a 22% closing ratio, this rep has little hope of meeting the objective. Moreover, during the summer months outbound cold calls had dropped dramatically because he was working on the written proposals. Had the rep spent his time on disqualifying the prospects, he'd have had more time to spend on true prospects.

How To Qualify

First, be direct. Tell the prospect what you plan to do. Use benefits so you don't sound too blunt. For example,

> "Mr. McMartin, I'm not sure if our product/service could benefit you but we have had considerable success with firms like yours in reducing their operational costs. In order to determine if we could save you some money I would like to ask you a few questions."

Prepare Your Questions, MAN

Have your qualifying questions prepared. Here's an acronym that might help you formulate your qualifying questions: **MAN**.

MAN refers to three critical components to qualifying. The **M** refers to money. You must determine if the prospect has the money to purchase your product, particularly if you sell a high ticket item. For example,

> "Ms. Scott, do you have money budgeted for this type of expenditure?"
>
> "Could funds be made available to finance the product?"

The **A** stands for authority. It is critical to know if you are dealing with a decision maker or an influencer. Don't be fooled by titles and position. Prospects can have a fancy, impressive title but be completely powerless in making a buying decision. One way to determine this is to ask "Ms. Authier, is there anyone else who will be involved in the decision to purchase?" Phrasing the question in such a manner is a polite but direct method of determining how much time should be spent with this individual.

Finally, the **N** refers to "need." This means, does the prospect have a potential need for the product or service? Clearly, significant thought must be placed here to frame the question.

Unlike the lead qualification, sales qualification does not have a limit to the number of questions that can be asked. The point is, determine the key questions that must be asked, list them and then use them as a guide.

Qualified or Disqualified?

At some point your qualifying process will yield a qualified or disqualified prospect. If the prospect is qualified, proceed with your sales cycle. While you may not get the sale, you will have at least bettered your odds.

If your prospect is disqualified, tell him. Directly. Don't beat around the bush or sugarcoat your reply. For example,

> "Based on what you have told me Mr. Craig, I don't think our product/service could provide a substantial benefit to you. I want to thank you for taking time in answering the questions."

Interestingly, the prospect is usually surprised that he or she was "let off the hook." Most appreciate your candor.

Warning! Some will be miffed that they somehow "did not qualify" and will ask you why. Be direct. For example,

> "Mr. Craig, you stated that your capital cost expenditures were already budgeted for the year and that there was no other funding possible."

If appropriate you might want to leave the door open:

> "Would you like me to give you a call when you are planning your budgets for next year?"

Far too many reps look upon a "no" from a prospect as rejection. It is not rejection. It is disqualification. Disqualifying a prospect is good, provided you have done a thorough job in the qualifying process. Qualifying prospects is the epitome of "working smarter, not harder." Learn to tightly qualify and watch your sales grow.

10

Are You Wasting Time Watering Dead Plants?

How much time should you spend following up with a prospect? I am talking about those prospects whom you have called and who have given you assurances that a decision is right around the corner. So you call, and call and call and call . . . and with each call you learn the prospect needs a little more time.

The question then becomes, are you simply watering a dead plant?

You see, some prospects will give you their assurance that a sale is pending simply because it is difficult for them to tell you otherwise. Some are nice guys who recognize that you have spent a lot of time on the project and they don't want to hurt your feelings. Other prospects haven't gotten around to it. In theory they have every intention of doing so, but never quite manage to muster the time or effort.

A Fear of Pushiness

What makes the situation difficult is that you feel convinced the prospect is just about there, you don't want to be too pushy and aggressive; you want to extend them a little more leash. But how long should that leash go? There comes a time when you must recognize that you might be wasting your time, and you're demoralizing yourself with every delay.

One solution is to be straightforward and put the prospect to task. For example,

> "Steve, I need your assistance. Over the past few
> weeks you have given every indication that the
> sale is a go. I guess I would like to know if there is
> an opportunity to do some business or perhaps
> the time is not quite right at this point?"

Shut up and wait for a response. Don't budge. Don't utter a sound.

Key Points

For this to work your tone must be sincere. There is a real danger that you might sound annoyed and you want to avoid that. That is why I suggest you ask for the prospect's help. In addition, you should give the customer an out (e.g. timing is not quite right). This phrase allows the customer to gracefully pull away; that alleviates some of the pressure he or she might harbor about hurting your feelings.

If the prospect says there is an opportunity do business, reply,

> "That's great Steve. We both have put a lot of time
> and effort into this project. When do you think
> we can get started?"

Press for a specific commitment. Don't hesitate to remind the prospect of the energy that has been devoted by the two of you. Otherwise you will sound selfish and petulant.

Watering a dead plant is not only a hopeless cause, it is a waste of precious water. Confronting the customer is never easy, but if you spend any measure of time with the customer, then you have earned the right to ask. Be a good gardener.

11

Are You Barking Up The Right Trees?

L eafing through some sales books, I discovered an interesting statistic common to a couple of texts: in just over 30% of all selling situations the prospect ends up not buying a product or service from *anybody*. I am not sure from where this stat was derived but gut tells me, it's probably accurate.

The useful implication is that if we can identify early on those people who have no real intention to buy, we can eliminate them from our call cycling and focus on those who have greater potential. In short, spend our time barking up the right trees!

How So?

In his book, *"Selling to the Top,"* David Peoples has developed an interesting principle:

> *Prospects will buy when there is a discrepancy between their perception of where they are and their opinion of where they should be.*

In other words, if prospects do not feel there is a discrepancy, they won't buy.

The trick, then, lies in determining if there is indeed a discrepancy. We do this by understanding the four possible states of mind for prospects.

State of Mind 1: Opportunity

In this scenario, the prospect recognizes that where she is now with any given product or service is not where her company/department/organization wants to be. The prospect has outgrown the existing products/ services that she is presently using and is looking for a change.

How do you recognize these prospects? Listen for phrases with the word "need" embedded here and there. For example.

> "What we really **need** is a quicker way of processing our claims."

> "We **need** someone who can show us the latest selling techniques for the high tech industry."

I love these words, don't you? They show you the client will buy because they recognize that their current situation will not allow them to do what they desire. Spend quality time with these individuals because they well definitely buy.

State of Mind 2: Problem/Danger

A slight variation on the above theme. This prospect realizes there is a discrepancy between where they are now and where they should be, but this is based on a crisis or problem. In terms of telephone sales listen for sentences like,

> "We're going to be in big trouble if we don't improve the rate of our claims processing. Customer satisfaction levels will drop like a stone."

Other words to key into are "crisis," "need for relief," "fix," and "danger."

The motivation is based on fear. Your chances of making a sale are pretty good. Spend time here.

State of Mind 3: "OKAY"

Here's where it gets hazy and where we waste far too much time. The prospect believes that his present situation is "okay." There is no discrepancy between where they perceive themselves now and where they should be. There is no apparent need or opportunity to tap. These prospects are relatively simple to identify because they tell you outright.

> "We're right on track in every department."

> "No. I don't see that as a concern."

You won't sell to these people. Everything may indeed be okay, or, they might perceive everything to be okay even if you don't. Either way, no sale. Don't waste your time.

By the way, I recognize that moving on is tough. I recently ran into a prospect who believed everything was okay in his shop. My probing revealed that he had a screaming need for assistance in at least two key areas. But no matter the direction I took, I was nipped in the bud. At first, I thought there was some hidden objection I was missing. Later I recognized that the prospect truly, honestly believed his shop was in tip-top shape. I moved on.

State of Mind 4: Too Good To be True

These guys drive me nuts. They believe their company/product is not only doing "okay" but actually doing better than they need to. They differ from the "okay" prospects, by the tone and passion in their voice and the words they choose.

And here's why. Not surprisingly, these are the people who personally made the decision to buy a product or use a service and feel this compelling need to overstate the results if only to justify their decision. They won't always tell you that they were the decision maker on the issue but you will recognize them by their conviction on their product or service:

> *"Are you kidding! This software does everything we want it to do and a heck of a lot more. We have customization capabilities that will allow us to grow for years to come. The warranty is iron-clad for five years. The service guys are the very best . . . yada, yada, yada."*

Even at the slightest hint that there may be something better or more effective, the "Too Good to be True" prospects will sweep down from the skies with vigorous denial.

These people won't buy. Not now. Not ever. Or this is until something causes them to move into state of mind #1 or #2. Or they get fired. It's a little sad. The key point: Don't waste their time, or yours.

Summary

Learn to listen to the tone of voice and the way prospects phrase their words. From this you will identify their state of mind, which, in turn, will help you identify where you should spend your time. The more time you spend selling to those who will buy, the more successful you will be.

Section Three: Effective Telephone Communication

12

How to Listen Your Way to More Sales

L istening can be tough. It is even tougher in the absence of face-to-face contact. Listening, however, remains the key to establishing a relationship with your clients. As the customer begins perceiving that you understand his world, relationships grow and sustain themselves. Here are some mistakes to avoid, and tips and ideas on how to improve your listening skills.

How Not to Listen

1. "I know this stuff."

Sometimes pre-call planning can work against you. Yes, you read that correctly. Occasionally reps overprepare. They feel they know so much about the client or the prospect that it builds a false sense of security.

Consequently, when a client provides information, there is a tendency to think, "I know that already." It is not so much that we entirely dismiss the comments made by the customer but rather we listen at 50%. We miss perspective. And when we miss the client's perspective we cannot fully comprehend their world.

2. "I can hardly wait to tell you that I know this stuff."

Similarly, when we're overprepared, we anxiously want to show the client how much we know. We want to impress her with our preparation. In this scenario we are waiting for the moment to tell the client what we know rather than listen to what she has to say.

3. "Let me tell you even more."

Sales reps are taught to listen for buying cues. Unfortunately, some reps simply wait for the cue so that they can use the opportunity to make their pitch. This is selective listening. There is a tendency to hear what we want to hear and then switch into the pitch mode. From that point on we stop listening.

What to Do to Listen More Effectively

1. Take notes. Taking notes forces you to concentrate on what the client has to say. It eliminates distractions around you because your mind is focused on the paper. As you take notes you have less of an opportunity to prepare rebuttals and pitches. Tell the prospect or client you are taking notes. They won't mind. In fact, most will be impressed, if not pleased:

> "Mr. Fontaine, I'll be taking some notes so I can assess your situation and not miss anything."

Telling him that you are taking notes also forewarns him that he might have to slow down or repeat himself. For example,

> "Dr. Maher, I didn't quite get that last bit of information concerning your use of trocars in surgery. I'm afraid my shorthand needs a little work. Could you go over that again?"

2. Ask Questions. Asking questions, of course, is the means of getting the client to speak. And that provides the opportunity to listen. There are several "generic"' questions that can assist in getting the client to open up. For instance,

> "Bob, I'm not quite sure what you meant by that last remark . . ."
>
> "Could you elaborate . . . ?"
>
> "Explain how that works . . ."
>
> "Can you go over that again . . . ?"

3. Provide a "playback." No amount of note taking and questioning will guarantee that you have listened or that you have listened and understood. The only way you can do this is by providing a playback or summary of what you have heard to your client:

> "So, Danny, let's see if I have this straight: You want to expand your market share by penetrating

the hospitals into the Northeast but you have yet
to find the personnel to implement the plan. The
strategy is further hampered by the fact that you
are virtually an unknown player in this area. Is
this correct?"

> **Tip:** It is vital that you simply don't repeat word
> for word what the client has said. That's
> "parroting." You must summarize and interpret.

One of three interesting things can happen when you provide feedback:

1) The client can confirm what you have played back:
"That's it, Ben. You've hit it right on the head."

2) The client can correct or modify your play back: "That's
not quite right, Ben. We do have two sales reps in the northeast already. Their focus has been only been on the hospitals in Boston."

3) The client can add more information:

> **Client:** 'Well, Ben, that summarizes it. I should
> also mention that we have the exclusive rights to
> the Graseby Pump from England. Typically, the
> pump can help reduce post operative costs by 30-
> 40%. Surgeons and hospitals are constantly look-
> ing for ways to reduce these costs. We have proven
> results and testimonials from Europe and here in
> the Midwest."

> **Sales Rep:** "So you see the pump as a unique
> means of penetrating the market despite the fact
> that your company is not well known. Am I get-
> ting the picture?"

Note the use of the last question. Don't be afraid to ask for
confirmation. Phrases like

> "How does that sound?", or,

> "Do I have it right?", or,

> "Am I on the right track?", or,

> "Is that correct on my part?", help check your lis-
> tening.

Listening helps you know the customer and his world. Another curious thing occurs: As you demonstrate your listening skills, the client gets to know *you* and *your* world. And the customer concludes you are reliable, trustworthy, and professional. That's what relationships are made of.

13

How to Communicate So Listeners Understand

I was monitoring calls the other day and was struck by the thought that communication, especially by telephone, is an awesome task. It isn't easy. I reached this not-so-stunning conclusion while listening to a rep make a presentation and then recognized that the prospect was totally confused and dumbfounded.

This got me thinking about some fundamentals of communications and how important it is to remind ourselves about what happens when we try to prospect and sell.

Here's a communications model.

Speaker ——— DISTRACTIONS ——— Listener
thought -words- filter   filter -words- thought

The Sender

The model reveals that the sender (sales rep) begins with a thought (the abstract thought of qualifying or selling, for instance). The rep then translates the thought into words (the "pitch") but before the message is delivered, it goes through a series of filters. By filter, I mean all the things that influence our behavior and approach to clients and prospects. Filters include things like our background, upbringing, education, and ethnic orientation. They shape our message. Another example of filtering is how we speak to others relative to their position, status, rank, etc. For example, the way we send the same message to a peer differs than the way we would send it to a subordinate, a spouse, a friend, a vice president, or to a customer or prospect. Filters can also be preconceived notions and thoughts about a company, a product, or an individual that can be favorable, neutral or negative. The point is, messages are filtered for dozens of different reasons.

After messages are filtered, there are distractions. Distractions (sometimes called "noise") refer to all those things that can interfere with the delivery and acceptance of a message. In telephone sales, by way of example, a distraction could be a bad connection. We can't hear well. A distraction could be a commotion going on around us or our prospect which annoys, distorts or detracts.

The Receiver

Once the message is sent, the receiver, who is also subject to distractions, hears the words then filters those words based on his or background makeup, position, and preconceived notions. The words are deciphered, and, ultimately, this leads to a thought, a notion, a perception, a belief, a conviction, or an objection.

What's the point? Lots can go wrong. Much of it uncontrollable. So, is the situation hopeless? No. We know that communication is imperfect. And we know that in telephone sales there are certain key areas where communication breaks down regularly. Therefore we can prepare strategies to counter the situation.

Five Key Areas

There are essentially five areas where communication between a sales rep and a prospect fall apart.

1. Opening Statements

If the prospect does not have a clear concise understanding of who you are and what you want, the subsequent message becomes garbled. State your name, your company, the reason for your call and a benefit. Write this down. (SCRIPT IT). Use it. Test it. Once you have it mastered, don't stray.

2. Questioning

Explain to the prospect that you are going to ask questions, why you are doing so, and what's in it for them. (SCRIPT IT). By following these steps you won't confuse the prospect. In essence, you are providing a road map for the next phase of your call.

3. Delivering a Sales Message

All products have features, advantages, and benefits. Create a Features-Advantages-Benefit sheet. If you like, create variations on how you describe the advantages and benefits and write them down. (SCRIPT IT). Modify if you like, but once you have captured the right mix of words, keep and use them.

4. Objections

Easily, 99% of all objections can be anticipated before you pick up the receiver. Create an objections chart. List the objections and write down your responses. (SCRIPT IT).

5. Closing

Many sales never close simply because the client wasn't asked. Create several closes. Write them down (SCRIPT IT). Practice them.

Keys to Effective Communication

- As you've noticed, the first key to effective communication is scripting. I am not talking about scripting an entire call word-for-word. I am talking about scripting word-for-word in certain key areas.

- Use the scripts. Not sometimes. Not usually. All the time.

- Eliminate distractions from your end of the call. Ensure your desk is in an area free from noise, traffic, etc. Turn your head away from all the commotion. If you don't use a headset, start now. Headsets reduce noise. While you can't eliminate distractions at the prospect's end of the call, you can listen for them. If you hear commotion or if the client seems to be distracted, comment on it. Ask if there is a better time.

Summary

Effective communication is an art and a science. There are some things you can control and others you can't. Work on the things you can and watch your sales grow.

14

How to Sound Great on the Phone

Placido Domingo, the opera star, has said, "My voice is my profession. My voice is my life."

The parallel to telesales is remarkable. When you think about it, your voice is your profession. Your voice is what paints a picture on the phone. The customer or prospect actually assesses your appearance by how you sound. This assessment may be on a conscious or subconscious level but make no mistake about it, you are being evaluated with every word you speak. It is vital, then, to groom your voice just as you would groom your appearance if visiting the customer's premise. Here are his ideas.

❏ **Do Facial Aerobics.** "Every morning I do aerobics," says Domingo. Facial aerobics, that is. He was referring to is a series of exercises that help limber up the vocal chords. It starts with sitting comfortably in a chair with your back straight and feet flat on the floor. Slowly begin by rolling your head in gentle and easy circles. This helps release tension. Reverse direction.

Then hunch up both shoulders and hold it to a count of five. Then do the same with the left and then the right. You should feel loosened and relaxed.

❏ **Yawn.** Next Placido opens his mouth slowly like he is having a slow, languorous yawn. It stretches the mouth and jaws. Do this several times. Each time you close your mouth, really pucker up. (This facial workout looks a little silly and usually generates a few bewildered glances and chuckles from co-workers. You might want to do this in private!)

❏ **Do a "Louis Armstrong."** Balloon your cheeks. Really stretch them. You will look and feel like a bullfrog. Strange, but fun.

Now you are limbered up. You can practice your script or review your outline several times to get your mouth used to saying the works. You will find that this warm up will give a little more zest to your presentations. Work will flow easier and you will experience less voice fatigue.

How to Work on Your Resonance

❏ **Hum.** Humming regularly and frequently gives your vocal chords a nice little work out. Apparently, the humming vibrates the vocal chords and this helps you get a more professional sounding resonance.

❏ **No Dairy Foods.** Avoid items such as ice cream, or milk or coffee creamer, or any other dairy products. These products tend to coat your throat and often forces you to hack or clear your throat.

Most of us are not blessed with great voices. Most of us squeak, squawk, boom, screech or whisper our way through life feeling that we are genetically stuck with what we've got. This need not be the case. Grooming your voice is simply a habit. It is a good habit. Remember, your voice is your profession.

I wonder what Placido would be like as a telesales professional.

15

How to
Sell the Sizzle

I gently placed the perfectly-seasoned Omaha Steaks on the grill. The symphony of hisses and pops coupled with the intoxicating aroma of dripping juices exploding on the white-hot coals put me into a trance. Thoughts drifted to one of my favorite subjects: sales. I recalled the old expression about sales-people selling the sizzle but not the steak. In other words, reps who talk a good product but fail to deliver the goods.

Any type of selling requires both the sizzle and the steak. However, the key ingredient in teleselling is the sizzle. I am going to assume that you do have a good product; that indeed, you "deliver." So let's concentrate on the sizzle.

"Sizzle" Defined

What is it? Webster's defines sizzle as "to be in a state of suppressed emotion or passion." It is that genuine enthusiasm we hear in a voice that tells us the person likes their job and they take pride in their company and their products or service; that they are confident and comfortable with what they are doing. It is something we sense and we know immediately when we hear it.

I heard it when I called to make reservations in Toronto. The reservationist took the necessary information in a friendly and efficient manner, and then asked if I was attending a function at the hotel. I was, and explained which one. "Oh," she replied with genuine interest, "that should be an exciting seminar judging by all the high-level executives attending like yourself."

Now, I am not a high level executive but I sure felt like one for the moment. She continued, "Did you know we have a special rate in the Executive Towers? You should see the rooms! They are *soooo* spacious and comfortable with a nice large work space," she chuckled and added, "in case you have homework."

The reservationist explained the price but also mentioned it included a buffet breakfast which she had tried and heartily recommended.

I have stayed in dozens of hotels across North America. Basically, they are generic, some more plush than others. But it was not so much what she said but rather how she said it. She truly believed the room—and all the amenities—were the best in North America.

I heard the confidence and I believed her. I booked into the Towers at a higher rate than I would have normally paid. Now that's sizzle!

Sizzle is more than telephone personality. Telephone personality is a skill that can be learned to help telesales pros perform better on the phone much in the same way that an actress or an actor learns acting skills to enhance their performance. But what is the difference between a great actor and a mediocre actor? Conviction. Belief. Lawrence Olivier was asked what made him so tremendous in a particular role. His reply was that he had a noble character with a noble goal and that he, Olivier, believed in that goal too. Sizzle.

Achieving Sizzle

How do you achieve sizzle? Learn about your product inside out. Try it and learn to believe in it. Clear up any doubts. Listen carefully to customer complaints about the product and feed that back to your manager. Offer improvement suggestions. In short, become part of the process. Make it your product and not just your company's. Take personal responsibility for its performance.

Sizzle is unlimited power when it comes to telesales. You will know it when you have it. And when you have it, selling the steak is easy.

16

It's the Same Old Song

While driving to a client's office I was tuned into my favorite radio station. They were playing a Motown classic that has the chorus,

"It's the same old song but with a different meaning . . ."

I've enjoyed that song for years, but in singing along with the melody, discovered I had forgotten most of the words. Encountering yet another traffic jam, it occurred to me that basic selling skills are not unlike old classics. We know the tune but the words are a little vague. Take listening. We know how important it is, but do we remember all the rules to enhance our listening skills?

A SPECIAL Formula

Here is a S.P.E.C.I.A.L way to reacquaint yourself with the "words."

Stop whatever you are doing. Stop eating, stop drinking, stop reading, stop writing up that last order. Often we overlap doing two jobs at once. Give 100% of your attention to the call.

Prepare to listen by grabbing a pen and paper, by accessing the customer's record, by having brochures, price lists, order forms, etc., at your finger tips. Don't lose your concentration by searching.

Evaluate what is said. Let the customer speak. Actively listen to determine the main points of a customer request or complaint. What are the hot buttons?

Concentrate on the message and not the message treatment. How often are you preparing a rebuttal to the customer's objection at the expenses of listening? As we mentally rehearse we fail to listen.

Investigate by questioning and verifying. Go back over the conversation and make sure you understand completely. Clarify confusing points.

Acknowledge the order or your understanding of an issue by repeating back to the customer, "So, as I understand it, Mr. Mason, you would like five cases of . . ." Leave no room for error.

Log everything by writing it down. (If there is a secret recipe to better listening, this is it.) This goes beyond completing an order slip. Make notes as you go along. They form an outline. They ensure that you won't forget.

17

Learning to Shut Up: The Power of Silence

M ost sales reps are unaware of the power that they can exert in a sales call by judiciously using silence. There are two reasons why you should use silence: one is obvious, the other not so.

Lets the Customer Talk

Here is the obvious reason. There is little point in asking a question if you have no intention of listening to the answer. This is so painfully obvious that I hesitate to comment further. Yet I think the vast majority of telesales pros dread a moment of silence in any customer contact—especially a cold call. I suspect that part of the reason is that sales reps are subconsciously worried that they will hear an objection, or worse yet, an unqualified rejection. Consequently they delay that inevitable moment of silence until they have run through their entire script. And even then, they seem hesitant to relinquish their hold on the conversation.

There seems to be an urge to spill everything in the hope that all possible objections will be preempted. In a way, it is a bizarre form of procrastination.

Rambling Raises Objections

Unfortunately, ironically, and, painfully, their endless ramblings only taint the entire presentation, probably raising more objections than they quell. By pausing and allowing the person to speak you can gather information. That much is blatantly obvious. But by using silence you get some added benefits. That moment of silence also allows you to collect your thoughts (and your breath!). It gives you a chance to be more cautious and thoughtful in your approach. Furthermore, silence lessens your chance of saying more than you mean to, want to, or need to.

Here is the less obvious reason why we use silence: Silence actually forces a customer to talk, even with those word-stingy customers who seem bent on making the life of a salesperson notoriously uncomfortable.

Silence in a conversation is like a vacuum or a void. It begs to be filled. When two people are engaged in a conversation there is typically a "my-turn-now-your-turn" pattern. In other words, when someone is finished speaking, they usually pause expecting you to make some sort of comment or affirmation. When you fail to pick up your end of the pattern, an uncomfortable silence ensues. Within seconds, you will find that the person will elaborate further.

Gathers More Information

In telesales, if a customer comes up with an objection or concern, try keeping your mouth shut. Do not comment. At the very most make a small "mmmmm. . ." You will discover that the customer finds the silence a tad uncomfortable and will launch into a more detailed explanation in only a second or two. And of course, once the customer starts to open up you will gather more information from which to base your reply.

Silence is truly powerful. Studies reveal that using silence denotes an air of wisdom and calm expertise. It suggests to the other person that you are an analyzer of facts. You don't shoot foolishly from the hip.

Do yourself a favor on your next call. Shut up and reap the benefits!

18

Listening: The Difference Between Persistence and Annoyance

A re you a persistent sales rep, or just plain annoying? The line between persistence and annoyance can be thin.

A case in point is a telesales rep who did a great sales job on me initially, but then pursued me until she has become a complete and utter pain in the behind.

A few years ago when I was with Bell Canada, Jennifer had initially sold me on the benefits of advertising in her company's weekly magazine. She presented a whole host of impressive studies claiming to have a well-balanced audience for my product. She handled my objections well and closed the sale.

I got four responses from the ad. Not great. Not necessarily her fault, but, nevertheless I was burned.

Jennifer continued to call seeking more advertisements, and her latest efforts included a rather impressive "independent survey" which probed the readers.

"It's your target, Jim," said she. "Shall I book you for a full page ad this time?"

"No," I replied emphatically, "You may not. The draw from my last ad to that well-targeted market only drew four responses. I doubt the survey and I plan to run another ad with XXX publication."

"Oh, they don't have the same readers as we do. Our survey shows it. It's not what you want."

"Then how come I pulled over a hundred orders with a single run?"

"Well, it's not who you should be targeting. The survey shows those that our publication is read more by your potential customers."

"Jennifer, you are not listening. I got four orders from your publication and over a hundred from XXX. Maybe your magazine isn't being read. Maybe your survey is not so accurate."

"Ah, but it's not 'our' survey. It was an independent survey. Take a look and see. It is our readers that should be buying your product?"

Need I go on? Jennifer was armed with a survey. It was both her shield and sword. She was so blinded by the "results" that her listening was obviously impaired. She bugged me with her innuendoes. For example, when she said, "It's not who you should be targeting", she was really saying, "Jimbo, you're wrong." That's a no-no.

Even so, I could forgive her momentary blindness. But she continued to call. Two more times and the conversation virtually repeated itself. What a pain. But to make matters worse, she managed to get through to my boss and his boss, who in turn came running to me, survey in hand, saying we should run an ad. Hey! Guess who got to break the news about the four lousy orders. I didn't look too good that day. It was something I was trying to keep quiet.

Lesson: Listen. Learn. Recognize a legitimate "no" and let sleeping dogs lie. Don't ruin a long run relationship for a short term kill.

19

Handling Sexist Remarks

A question I have encountered is, "What do I do when I encounter sexists remarks?" Obviously, this is a tender issue that affects female salespeople and it is one that is usually ignored because of its sensitive nature. Yet it is an issue that can blow your whole day, and your presentation. So what should you do?

Three Options

The following strategies are ideas garnered from females who have attended my training sessions and have firsthand experience with this issue. Here are three options.

1. Ignore it. Gauge the nature of the remark. Is it blatantly sexist or mildly so? In the case of the latter, give the customer the benefit of the doubt; you may have misinterpreted. Even if it is fairly obvious, try ignoring it. Usually the offender will quickly get the message that you can't be harangued. Be aware that there are, and always will be, chauvinists. Understand that this mentality has a lot to do with the way the individual was raised, where he was raised, his age, maturity and the like. Getting upset with the customer will not change this. Understand too, that there is a chemistry between men and women. There can be sort of "jockeying" in any male/female encounter. Call it flirting, if you like. It is not usually meant to be offensive but rather a way of establishing relationships. For example, if you are asked to meet for a drink, you might want to say "Sure, can I bring my husband (or boyfriend) along." This establishes the playing field.

Also understand that some customers and prospects will throw out sexist remarks as some kind of bizarre test to see if you can be "one of the boys." If you take it good-naturedly, you pass, and chances are you won't be subjected to the remarks again. If you don't . . . well . . . who knows?

2. Challenge it. Inevitably, there are remarks that are downright offensive. A good way of challenging the individual is to calmly remark,

> "Excuse me, Mr. Prospect/Customer, would you mind repeating that? I am taking notes."

There is something powerful about the "written word." The thought of his remarks appearing in print somewhere might be embarrassing for the customer to contemplate. There is a danger, of course. The customer may become defensive, or even more offensive. Challenges have a way of doing that.

3. Hang up. If the remark is blatant and you can't ignore it and you are not up to challenging it, simply terminate the call.

This issue is constantly evolving, so if you have additional ideas, please let me know.

20

Words That Maim And Kill: Part I

As if selling by phone isn't challenging enough, some reps feel compelled to make their jobs even more difficult. They use words that can maim and kill a sale.

Here are examples I heard when call-monitoring. While you may get a chuckle or two when you read them, there are some important lessons to be learned.

Sales-Killing Examples

❑ **Blame it On the Season.** "I guess it's probably hectic; it being Christmas. How about I call you in the new year some time?" The telesales rep manufactured a ready-made excuse! Which is sad, because I have found Christmas can be a good time to sell (year-end budgets, tying up loose ends etc.)

❑ **Seasonal Favorite II.** "My bet is that you don't want to buy at this time of year." And to show his flexibility in delivery: "I know if it were me, I'd want to think about it."

❑ **Doubting Thomas.** "I doubt if you would be interested in reviewing the upgraded version of this (product), right?"

❑ **Doubting Thomas II.** This sales rep actually created the doubt she was so worried about: "It's really a good policy but I must tell you that it doesn't come with accidental death coverage." The operative word was "but." This rep hoisted a red flag in the prospect's mind, and guess what? No sale. Suddenly the accidental death coverage became an issue.

❑ **Mail It Again.** "Ok, you haven't received our mailer yet? How about I send you another?" A good example of wasted postage, wasted telephone call and wasted breath. (I think this rep actually scripted this line for she used it no less than 11 times in two hours.)

❑ **Blame it On the Product.** "Our product people simply don't know how to design a product that fits the needs of store owners like you."

❑ **Blame it On Another Department.** This is very popular. I have several examples of it. "I don't think there's a hope in hell that you'll get a deviation on the price from our underwriters." Tell me: who would buy from a company so fraught with internal strife?

Another: "Boy," said the rep, "If I had a nickel for every time I heard that complaint about the busy lines in our customer service department."

Here is a similar example, "I wish our delivery time was better but there's nothing I can do about it. They're understaffed." Some reps consider it a badge of courage to reveal the company's flaws. It's as though the rep's honesty some how prevails over the problem.

❑ **Give a Reason to Object.** "Well our terms are not the greatest but you can't argue about the price."

And to show you that infections can spread, here's what the guy next to him had to say, "Unfortunately, while the plan has a good price it does not cover scaling." What makes this pathetic is that the prospect had no idea what scaling was. Dutifully, the caller explained the procedure and assured the client it was a vital ingredient. When asked if there was a policy that covered scaling the rep coolly replied, "Well yes there is but you will have to pay lot more in premium." Should I even bother to comment?

❑ **"Let Me Finish!"** In one call the prospect objected with "I am not really interested." To which the rep indignantly replied "Hey wait a minute, I'm not done yet."

Gee, what more can I add?

And the list could go on. At this point you might think that these examples are taken from inexperienced, burned out, or "loser" reps. Not so. While some clearly lacked skill and finesse, there were other very good sales reps who subtly slipped the knife into their own backs. It is an example of how we can be our own worst enemies.

What To Do?

Now is as good as time as any to create a list of resolutions that are designed to stamp out words that can maim and kill our customers:

1. Tape your calls for the next two weeks. Not for a day or two, but for the next two weeks. Anything less and you won't get a good feel for your 'darker' habits. Review them with a co-worker, or better yet, a supervisor. Listen for killing words. Determine why you used them. Jot them down daily.

2. Have your supervisor monitor your calls. Regularly. And get feedback so you don't lapse into your old behaviors.

3. Review your script or call guide. Are you following it or have you strayed from it? Review your objections sheets and product information sheets. Are you following them or have you 'improvised' along the way?

4. If you don't have them already, create them. I have long been an advocate of scripts and call guides to help ensure call quality.

5. Improve product knowledge and sales skills. Ask for information and/or look for sources (books, newsletters, videos etc.) that will improve your expertise.

6. Note customer concerns. You do this for two reasons. One, to see if there really is a problem or did you simply make it up in your mind? You might find that the number of times you hear the objection/concern does not warrant your attitude. And two, if there is numeric proof, you have the evidence to take to your customer service department, product people, manager or whoever so that they can fix it.

7. Listen to others in your department. Try to determine if they use words that maim and kill. It gives you good perspective.

21

Words That Maim and Kill Part II: The Sales Rep

In the previous chapter we talked about how sales reps use words with clients/prospects that can actually kill or maim any chance of a sale. Now we'll look at words reps use when speaking to themselves, their peers, or anyone else who happens to be listening.

The following example is taken from a real life incident in a call center. It is typical of many salespeople.

The rep explained to me in a coaching session, "We can never beat them on price."

So what's already wrong? The rep had not even picked up the phone that morning. Yet he had painted a picture of defeat in his mind.

It's tragic. Before they utter a word to a client or prospect they have already polluted their minds with reasons why people won't buy. With that type of thinking, it's easy to see why reps feed their clients a steady diet of "don't-buy-from-me"-type feelings.

"Yeah, But"

The interesting thing is that when you try to logically deal with this type of attitude, some people will actually go out of their way to defend their negative tendencies. They invariably use the "yeah-but" defense. For example, with one rep I said,

"Price is often a key factor in a proposal. So if price is the motivator why not offer the Value Plan?"

"***Yeah***, the Value Plan is cost effective, ***but*** it does not include scaling. (a teeth cleaning procedure for pets)"

"Is scaling important to the customers?" I inquired.

"Well, I am pretty sure it is. Most customers find it important."

"Did you ask? Was this identified as a need?"

"No."

I replied, "Let's take a different approach. The Elite Plan offers scaling. If scaling is so important to the client, why not offer it?"

"***Yeah, but*** the Elite Plan includes disability?"

"So???" I ask.

"Well, clients don't want disability."

"Oh I see," said I. "Did you ask?"

"No."

"Isn't disability a good thing to have?"

"***Yeah, but*** it increases the premium and when I tell the client about the disability it turns them off."

I can't bear to go any further. The rep was building ready-made excuses for not selling the product. He lost before he had even begun calling.

Apart from maiming his mind by his negative words, there are a couple of other factors contributing to this negative attitude. First, the rep made broad assumptions. He assumed that all clients thought scaling was important. As it turns out, most of the clients had no idea what scaling was. Secondly, armed with these false assumptions, the rep did not bother to question to determine the client's needs.

There's more. In cases where scaling was deemed important, the rep felt compelled to position the disability coverage as an unnecessary add-on which raised the price. In fact, the rep actually told clients that the Elite plan included scaling but also included disability. Of course the clients viewed it as a negative simply because the rep positioned it as one.

This it a classic example of talking too much. If disability is unimportant to the client, then don't sell the feature of disability. If scaling is important, sell the scaling feature and its benefits.

Where the "Yeah, Buts" Came From

Shortly after the conversation with this rep I met with five or six other salespeople for coffee. These guys were the "grizzled old vets."

It was deja vu. I heard the same dialogue as I had with the rep that morning about scaling!

We tend to build "support" groups that reinforce our attitudes. Sometimes we fall into the trap of hanging out with negative individuals. Over a period of time, a subtle brainwashing occurs. We actually begin believing our own negative junk and spread it to our clients.

What to Do

1. The next time you're with a bunch of reps, stop and listen. How do they speak? How do they position your product or service? Is it negative or positive? Is there a pattern forming? Figure out if those around you jump on the bandwagon.

2. If it is a negative atmosphere try to determine if there is any legitimacy to it. If there is a product flaw of some sort, do the proper people in management know about it? And it is simply not enough to "mention" it. Anyone can do that. Go further. Gather data. Collect "evidence." For example, when I asked the reps how many clients/prospects actually mention scaling, there were only two out of several hundred who had commented. And make some suggestions or recommendations.

3. If there is no legitimacy to the whining or complaining, then remove yourself from that environment. Don't hang out with that crowd. It will poison you.

4. If you find that you are already poisoned with negative talk, stop it. You have a choice. Learn more about the product features and benefits. Spice up your selling skills by reading newsletters, read sales books, listen to selling and motivational tapes.

Words that maim and kill a client evolve from the same words we speak to ourselves. Keep a keen ear out for how you speak to yourself and others. Ensure it's all positive, and your thoughts and actions follow.

22

Your Voice: The Vehicle On Which Your Message Travels

Your voice is the primary medium of communication between you and your prospects and customers. But how much time do you devote to ensuring that the medium is the very best that it can be?

I am sure many of you are aware of a UCLA study which looked at how people communicate thoughts, feelings, and ideas. The study showed that face-to-face, 55% of our message is communicated by body language, 38% by our tone and only 7% by the words we use.

When we communicate by phone, however, the body language is eliminated and it is estimated that anywhere from 80-90% of our message is communicated by our tone and the remainder by words.

While these numbers surprise most people, they do present opportunities. By developing and enhancing your voice, you're able to not only make a significant impact on the prospect or customer but also to differentiate yourself from your competitors (who likely have bland and mediocre voices).

Let's take a look at how your voice can impact the listener and then we'll look at what you can do to improve it.

When we speak to prospects for the very first time, their minds are a blank void, a hole in space, a vacuum. Vacuums beg to be filled and the moment you utter a sound, the prospect paints a picture of what you look like. What's import here is to understand that the prospect evaluates you on both a conscious and (very importantly) subconscious level. This evaluation often determines whether or not they will listen further, much less buy.

Here are some problems that plague many telephone sales reps.

Volume

Have you every encountered a prospect with a loud, booming voice? What image do you paint? Typically, loud voices are associated with a pushy, aggressive and domineering individual. Do you like these people?

Most of us don't. If you have a loud voice, prospects create an image of you and your company that is less than flattering. Most don't buy because they feel they are being "pushed."

On the other hand, have you every dealt with someone who has a soft voice? Someone you can barely hear? Not only is it annoying to have to press the telephone to your ear to hear them but you also get the impression that the person is perhaps incompetent. Soft voices conjure up images of people who are uncertain. And of course, if you are a rep with a soft voice, it could be the kiss of death. The prospect won't be confident with your recommendations.

And the worst thing is that the client may not even make this judgement on a conscious level. Subconsciously, the message has a negative effect.

Rate

A fast talker usually makes us feel that either he is rushed or that he is rushing us. Often I hear the rate of a call increase late in the day as telephone reps rush to meet their quota. Invariably, they do not make any sales.

The reason is simple. The average person does not trust a fast talker because there is a feeling that he or she is trying to pull the wool over our eyes. No trust = no sale.

A slow talker can have the same effect on a sale. Like a low-volumed talker, a slow talker gives one the impression that the rep is reading a script. That implies that the rep is inexperienced and unsure of himself. A slow talker plods along and bores the prospect. The slow talker does not inspire confidence. No sale.

Tone

Tone refers to how we say something. It is not a matter of what we say that makes the impact but rather how we say it.

Tone refers to a number of components such as inflection, intonation and rhythm. Collectively they create character and personality. The way we inflect and intonate gives the words added meaning. For example,

> "Dr. Ross, I really **believe** the Graseby Infusion Pump can make a significant **impact** on your patients' recovery."

Injecting personality makes you more believable. Inflecting and intonating create a certain degree of passion and conviction in your presentation.

By varying your rhythm and rate, you force the client to listen closely. Listen to James T. Kirk (Star Trek) or John Wayne when they deliver their soliloquies. You will hear them pause, speed up and slow down. This break in rhythm is unusual. And because it is unusual it gets the listener's focused attention.

Accents

Accents can be a touchy topic; they can work for or against you. If the accent is too pronounced, it sometimes gets in the way of the message. The prospect either is listening to the accent or they are trying to understand what you are saying.

On the other hand, if the accent is a little more subtle, chances are the prospect will listen closely. They do this because the accent is unusual. The accent can help differentiate the sales rep from all the rest of the sales reps who call this prospect. (I have had some very creative and talented reps who have actually tried a variety of accents when delivering messages and found their success rate improved significantly even though the script was never once altered).

Mannerisms

Culture, education, background, geography . . . all these factors can contribute to mannerisms in our speech patterns. As a Canadian, I am sometimes labelled with the "Bob and Doug Mackenzie" mannerism of saying "eh" at the end of a sentence.

Mannerisms, like accents, can work for or against you. Too pronounced and they become distracting. Used occasionally, they work in your favor by creating personality.

Jargon

Though not specifically voice-related, industry jargon can be a curse in your delivery. It can make you sound pompous if you are not careful. And, more importantly, it can confuse the prospect. You see, not all prospects are familiar with jargon. But what is worse, most of them will not tell you that they don't understand. Rather than look foolish or uneducated, they remain silent. Of course, the bottom line is, the vast majority won't buy simply because your message was crammed with clutter.

So these are some of the things that can impact your voice. The trick is to be aware of them and alter your approach.

How do you do this? Well, you need a tape machine, a good supervisor and an open mind. Tape your calls and have the supervisor or trainer listen to them. Get their feedback and impressions. If there are changes to be made, accept them with the recognition that no one has ever taught us to use our voices in an effective manner. Implement the changes and practice them.

23

Improving the Quality of Your Voice

It sounded like fingernails dragging excruciatingly slowly across a blackboard. Actually, it was Jeff, a telesales rep. "I am stuck with the voice I have. It's a genetic thing," he complained to me.

But despite that shivering sensation creeping down the back of my spine as I monitored his calls, I simply replied "You are not stuck with the voice you have. You can improve it with a little training and practice."

Most telephone reps don't have a bad voice like Jeff. It's just that most reps don't have a very *good* voice. The vast majority of telephone reps simply have a mediocre voice. Which ultimately makes them like everyone else who uses the telephone as a sales and marketing tool. Giving you one heck of an opportunity to differentiate yourself from the pack.

Here are some tips on how to improve the quality of your voice. If you implement them and practice on a regular basis, you will develop an edge over your competitors. You will also see a marked improvement on your calling results.

There are two elements to creating a superb voice: physiological and psychological.

Physiological

1. Hum. Yes, I know I mentioned this in a previous chapter. So do it. Hum in the shower, hum in the car, hum in the mall, hum in the call. Everywhere. Humming vibrates your vocal chords. Gives them a real work out. And as they vibrate they become stronger. As they become stronger your base in your tone becomes deeper and more resonant. The deeper your voice the more authoritative you sound. This helps create a sense of confidence in your listener.

2. Exercise Your Face. Not unlike a warm-up before a big game, having a "facial workout" will loosen the muscles around your throat and jaw. Start by tightening your face and clenching your teeth. Then relax. Repeat this several times.

Another good exercise is to yawn. By that I mean open your mouth as wide as you can. Feel it stretch. Close it and do it three or four more times. You will feel it in your jaw and your skin. Feels good too.

3. Loosen Your Neck and Shoulders. Next, tense your neck and shoulder muscles. Bunch them up and relax. Do this several times. Raise and lower your shoulders a few times.

4. Give Your Lungs a Workout. Take a few deep breaths and hold the breath for 10-20 seconds and then exhale. This expands the lungs. It stretches and strengthens the lungs. By having strong lungs your voice will sound less fatigued and strained.

5. Read Aloud. Do it at home for ten to fifteen minutes a day. Again, it strengthens your vocal chords. Makes them more robust.

6. T.A.L.K. Bill Stephens, a noted disc jockey has a little formula that he teaches rookie DJ's. He uses the T.A.L.K. program.

T stands for "tape" yourself. Read out loud and tape yourself as you go. Review it. Listen and monitor your tone, rhythm, pace and volume.

A refers to "articulate" which means when you do read out loud take the time and articulate the words. Be thorough. Pronounce each clearly. Not only does it strengthen your facial and vocal muscle, it improves your presentation skills.

L means "listen." Listen to the professional actors, DJ's, and newscasters. Note how they form and deliver their words.

K means "Keep disciplined." All the recommendations so far are so simple and easy that it is tempting to believe they won't do a lot for you. Wrong. Stick to it. Don't get lazy.

One thing Bill recommends is taking a print ad from a magazine or newspaper and reading and taping it aloud. Then he suggests imagining yourself as a football coach. Pretend you are in the locker room before the big game against Notre Dame. Read the words from the print ad but recite them as a coach might. Do the same thing but pretend you are a priest or a minister. The exercise forces you to deliver the words in a different manner. It's fun and funny. And it is so powerful because it shows you how you can manipulate your voice. Try it. Fun at parties too.

7. Straighten Up! There's more. When you are at your desk, sit straight up. Don't slouch. You breath from your diaphragm. If you are slouched you place pressure on the diaphragm and your lungs to get enough air. The effect is not unlike letting the air out of a balloon slowly. You get the squeaky, often embarrassing little noise.

8. Stay Loose. Don't wear tight collars or clothes.

9. Garbage In, Garbage Out. Watch what you eat and drink. Warm liquids help lubricate your throat. But watch out for liquids like cream or milk. These can coat your throat forcing you to clear your throat. (Incidentally, clearing your throat too often suggests to the average listener that you are not telling the truth.) And please, for heaven's sake, avoid carbonated drinks. You know as well as I do that they make you burp or hiccup. And don't chew gum or eat.

Psychological

On a psychological level, keep a gauge on negative events. They can have a significant impact on your voice. We are literally bombarded with negative messages on a daily basis from the newspapers, radios and television. We listen to friends and co-workers moan and complain about their partners, their job, their kids, their neighbors and their pets. And then, after all this, we sit at our desk and begin calling. It is little wonder our voice may lack a certain degree of enthusiasm.

Now let's look at the opposite. Before you sit down and make those calls, why not take a few moments and visualize positive events. One exercise that seems to have a very positive effect is something I call the "Lotto." Of course a lotto is a draw for money. I suggest to reps that the lotto is worth 14.4

million dollars (no more and no less) and that their numbers have just been drawn. Think about the freedom. The possibilities. The fun. The excitement! Do that for about 30 seconds or so and watch what happens when you pick up the phone to make your first call.

Most reps state they feel pumped. The adrenaline is flowing. And ultimately, there is a direct correlation to those thoughts and to how we sound to the customer or prospect. They hear someone who is upbeat and positive.

Let your voice do the work for you.

Section Four: Call Openings That Create Interest

24

Scripting The Opening Statement

The first 15-20 seconds of any phone call are the most critical. It is here that the mood and tone of the conversation is set. It is here that the customer or prospect will decide whether or not to listen further. That's why opening statements should be scripted word-for-word.

Simple Rules

1. State Your Full Name

This is a no-brainer. However, countless times I have monitored calls where the name is completely omitted, or, at best, the first name only is supplied. This is particularly so on follow-up calls to existing clients and prospects. Stating your full name is professional. Anything less is not.

Incidentally, it is a good scripting idea to start by stating the client's or prospect's name. This ensures you have the correct person on the line. And, when people hear their name, they tend to listen to the next couple of sentences very closely . . . which is exactly what you want.

2. State Your Company Name

Common sense, you say? Believe me, there is still a huge market for common sense. Let the customer or prospect know where you are calling from. If you are not readily known, you might have to add a rejoinder such as "We specialize in . . ."

3. State the Reason for Your Call

Ah, here is where the rubber meets the road and scripting begins to fall apart. Too often, reps get involved in long-winded explanations that totally overwhelm and confuse the prospect or customer. Here is a scripting hint that helps keep you on track. Start this part with, "The reason for my call is . . ." This forces you to focus on the specific call objective and/or the offer that should have been developed in the pre-call planning stage. This simple, though perhaps unimaginative little phrase also lets the customer know exactly where you want to go. It clears the clutter.

Of course, a certain amount of tact must be used. For instance, starting a cold call with "The reason for my call is to sell you product X . . ." is not a good idea. That is why you must do your homework.

4. Add a Benefit Statement

This tells the prospect why he or she should listen further (i.e., what's in it for them). It's absolutely critical for first-time calls. In some cases though, it could be optional. For example, if you have established a rapport with certain customers over a period of time, a benefit statement is often implied and understood. In other words, you can be more direct. (This is often another good time to insert the client's/prospect's name again.)

Let's look at an example of everything tied together:

> "Hello Mr. Charendoff. I'm John Newbold with Cybermation. We specialize in automation software for MVS and Distributed environments. Mr. Charendoff, the reason for my call is that we've had considerable success in reducing scheduling costs with companies like JC Penney and Nike, and I was wondering if I could take a few moments of your time to see if there's a possible fit."

Tips

At this point in the scripting process, there are a few tips.

1. Don't sit down and begin to "write the script." Sit down, jot a few notes such as the call objective/and offer to act as a guide.

2. "Speak" the words. The way we speak and the way we write are two different breeds of cat. If you begin to write too soon, you will get caught up in editing well before the creative process has been completed.

3. Have a tape recorder close by, and keep it on "RECORD." It is amazing how someone in the group will suddenly find the right mix of words. Capture them on tape instead of trying to transcribe them onto paper.

25

Scripting: Building Your Call Road Map

Once you have developed your opening statement, the next step is to put yourself in your customer's or prospect's shoes. The objective is to anticipate all of the responses that the customer/prospect could create. For example,

> "Ms. Taylor, this is Sue Ferarzi calling from Pet Plus Insurance. The reason for my call is to follow up on our conversation last week where we discussed the health insurance for your Golden Labrador. I'd like to go through the brochure I sent you to point out the highlights of the plan you indicated you had interest in."

Three Possible Attitudes

Ms. Taylor can only possess one of three attitudes at this point: acceptance, indifference, or objection. You simply have to translate those three attitudes into possible responses. For example, acceptance is "Yes, I want to buy right now," or, "Yes, I'm interested, let's go through it." Indifference is a stall such as "I'm busy right now, can you call me back later," or, "I need to think about it further." Indifference also includes "no." And finally, objections show up as questions about the product or price, or any other question or concern about the product or service.

If we know the attitudes and can anticipate the precise customer/prospect replies, we can build appropriate responses for each. If you did such a great job on the previous call that the response is "I would like to enroll," you can immediately flip into an order processing mode. If they are prepared to grab the literature and go through it with you, you would be ready with your questioning for this call. If you hear things like "I would like to think about it," you can respond accordingly.

To make the process easier, I recommend developing a "road map" using "defaults." After scripting your opening statement draw a guide, something like the illustration below.

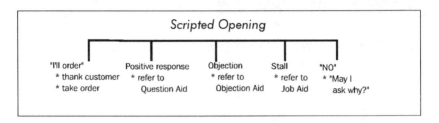

Scripted Opening

"I'll order"	Positive response	Objection	Stall	"NO"
* thank customer	* refer to	* refer to	* refer to	* "May I
* take order	Question Aid	Objection Aid	Job Aid	ask why?"

Beneath each customer response you can list your replies as I have done. Note that in the "I'll order" response I have used bullet-point form to direct the call. In the next three I refer to job aids where there will be other scripted responses. And finally with the "no" response I leave a word-for-word reply for the rep to use.

Tips

•**Use the Defaults.** This saves you time and quickly plots where you are and want to go in the call.

• **Use oversized paper.** I use 11 x 17 sheets and "cut and paste" my replies. This gives plenty of room to see the entire picture and saves the hassle of flipping back and forth.

• **Use highlighters to track various responses.** I have one rep who uses green for "yes" and another color for "no." He says it is like highlighting various routes on a road map; it makes navigating the trip fast and simple.

26

Four Reasons to Not Use AHAYT

("And How Are You Today?")

In the first week home from my vacation I had no less than seven different telephone sales calls ... from home improvements to freezer package deals, from the Heart Fund, to the local youth summer athletic program. All these calls differed in their style, content, script format, and presentation. However, they did have one identical characteristic: every call I took came up with "and how are you today?" (or AHAYT for short).

I think it stinks.

And what is more, I believe we should band together to stamp out that most insipid of telemarketing/telesales phrases. We could wear buttons that say "I hate AHAYT." Prospect would like it and I suspect the vast majority of sales reps who are forced to use it would cheer as well.

Pardon my cynicism, but by the fourth or fifth call, the moment I heard those words, something clicked inside, something turned off. I was no longer listening to the message, but rather I was preoccupied with annoyance. And then it dawned on me that every call I could ever remember contained that silly "non-sequitur." I don't think I am alone when it comes to these sentiments.

Here are four reasons why you should avoid the phrase.

1. It is not sincere. I don't care what you say, after ten or fifteen calls, it flows automatically from your mouth not from your heart.

2. It lacks imagination. Surely, there has to be a better way to break the ice. Anyone who develops a script with AHAYT in it is just plain lazy. Boring!!

3. It doesn't break the ice. In fact it thickens it. Let's face it, as soon as these words are uttered, a frown furrows its way on the brow of the prospect. You haven't even begun your presentation and he or she has their guard up.

4. It invites responses you do not want. Suppose someone replied, "Well, I have a splitting migraine headache you wouldn't' believe." What would you say after a retort like that?

5. It is stupid (bonus reason).

An AHAYT isn't designed to inquire about health and well being. Supposedly, it is designed to make you, the sales rep feel good. It is designed to get people to say "good" or "fine." The theory is that it puts people in a "positive" mode.

Exceptions?

OK. I am being a bit fanatical. There are some times when AHAYT is acceptable.

First, if there is a prior relationship with the customer (be it at a consumer or business-to-business level), by all means ask him or her how they are. It is a natural greeting between acquaintances. But the operative word here is "acquaintances." When you speak with someone you know, asking them how they are is more than just a "filler." It is a sincere inquiry about their health and well-being. It establishes and enhances rapport. And herein lies the difference.

Second, "If it ain't broke, don't fix it." If you are the rare individual who is sincerely concerned about a stranger, by all means, use the phrase. Don't let me stop you. On the other hand, if you did not use the phrase, would your orders or leads increase further?

Summary

Asking how the prospect/customer is doing is OK when there is a prior relationship. I said "OK," not great. When there is no prior relationship it is a waste of time and breath.

27

Opening Statement Fundamentals

Two sales rep trainees were role playing. I eavesdropped as they tried developing their opening statements. They struggled, and their results showed. This incident served to remind me that we should review some basic fundamentals of opening statements and then add a variation that might be new to you.

The Fundamentals

I know we already covered openings in a previous chapter, but let's revisit the basics. Dissect a good opening statement and we find that it consists of three parts.

1. Identify Yourself and Your Company

It seems so simple, but still it is neglected at times. This is especially true if you are new to telephone selling. Rookie sales reps are often so anxious to get to their call that they often forget to identify themselves and/or their company.

Yet the value of this remark should not be lost on the veteran reps either.

Look at one I received:

> "Hi Jim. Hey, I've got the quote you wanted on those promotional pieces. On a batch of 100 the cost is $257.00 with tax. So, is it a go?"

My mind was a million miles away at the time and I had no idea to whom I was talking. Being polite, I listened to the voice rather than the information that was being provided. When I finally tuned into the voice and recognized who it was, the vital information was lost. I was forced to ask him to repeat the numbers again. Sadly, this came from a rep with thirty-two years sales experience.

2. State the Reason for Your Call

"Mr. Mason, this is Chris Vandervan of Goldlinks Promotional Inc., specialists in high quality motivational products. The reason for the call is to determine if we can be of help to your company."

In this example, I know who is calling and why. But there is one more critical element.

3. State the Benefit

Here is a variation to most benefit statements. I call it "The Humble Approach."

Before your call, ask yourself: If I were the customer, why would I listen further? What is the potential benefit? Here is an approach that you might find beneficial.

"Ms. Warren, this is Lisa Allen calling from *Enterprising Women, Inc.*, the magazine for business women in North America. Ms. Warren, I do not know if taking an ad out in our magazine would interest you but a number of companies, similar to yours, have had tremendous response and sales as a result of their ads in *Enterprising Women.* I would like to ask you a few questions to see if you might benefit as well . . ."

I like this opener because it is unusual and it is subtle. On the one hand, it is unusual because Lisa is humble. She does not know if the ad would be of "interest" to Ms. Warren. To admit this fact is a unique approach because it acknowledges the customer's need to feel special. Sometimes sales reps are a little too presumptuous in their approach. For example, "Mr. Syberg, I can save you 20% on your advertising budget" is folly. How do you know you can save 20% unless you have access to information concerning Syberg's budget? I do not want to take anything away from a self-confident approach, but it should be acknowledged that most customers will erect a defensive wall in order to "not be sold." The "I don't know . . ." helps crack that barrier.

On the other hand, Lisa does not wimp out simply because she does not know if Ms. Warren has an interest or not. Subtly she ties in the fact that others (perhaps, competitors!) are using ad space in the magazine.

But wait! There's more. Lisa adds a strong benefit statement by making reference to the response and the sales that it generates. She concludes the opening statement by directing Ms. Warren into the questioning phase of the sales call.

Triple Benefits

In essence, the customer is hit with a triple whammy:

1. An unusual opening which will get her listening more closely.

2. The customer's curiosity is piqued by a reference to businesses "similar to hers."

3. There is the benefit of increased sales.

Final Tips

Okay now, some final tips. Make sure you have the evidence to support your claim. Refer to the other businesses by name. Heck, if they are buying advertising space, it is not a secret once the magazine is out. And if you have response rates that you can quote without breaking client confidentiality, use them.

Try this one on for size.

28

How to Develop Your "What We Do" Statement

Here's quick test. You are at a business luncheon and are speaking with one of the attendees (in fact, a potential prospect). He asks who you work for. You tell him. Then he says, "Oh, what do they do?" Quick, now, write your reply:

_____

_____

_____

If you are like most sales reps, you will struggle through this exercise . . . maybe coming up with something . . . only after considerable thought and editing. And if it is your first attempt, it is likely not very good. Don't fret, though. We'll work on it together.

One of the most important elements of an opening statement in a cold call is developing a brief statement which succinctly describes what your company does. I call the a "WWD" or a "What we do" statement.

A "WWD" is one of those small, but oh, so critical, components of an opening statement that is often overlooked. And when it's overlooked, problems arise.

The Problem

In most prospecting scenarios, the sales rep calls, introduces herself, her company and the reason for the call plus a benefit statement. Sounds good doesn't it? Unfortunately, if the prospect is not familiar with your company, the reason for the call and the benefit statement are lost in the clutter and confusion.

You see, while you are you rattling on about the benefits you might bring to the organization, your prospect is back at stage two. She is trying to figure out who your company is and what relevance it has to her. What that really means is that she has either stopped listening completely or is listening with half an ear.

The Solution

If you want to have greater success in prospecting and cold calling you must be more effective and more powerful in your opening statement. To do this you must provide a reference point relative to your company. By doing so, you will get your prospect to listen more carefully to your reason for your call and the benefits that you have to offer.

Your objective is to build a concise and focused description of what your company does. The operative word is concise. Too long, and you bore or turn off the prospect. Too short, you leave them confused.

Here's How You Do It

Start building your WWD statement by having a group workshop with your fellow associates. Get everyone to quickly write what they think your company does. Review the statements together.

Be prepared for the shock. You might think that you all work for a different company.

Next scan or review your company literature (letters, brochures, bulletins, etc.) Is there anything that clearly describes what your company does? Compare and contrast the literature to the descriptions that you and your associates have listed.

Evaluate all the material. And here's the secret. Position yourself as a prospect. All too often, companies describe themselves in as self-serving manner. I don't mean this critically, but sometimes companies get so focused on what they do that they forget to describe the company in a manner that is meaningful to the customer or prospect.

Ask yourself "What is it that a prospect needs to hear to

understand what we do?" From that perspective, develop the words.

Here is a template that can help you get started.

"I'm calling from (your company name). *We specialize in* _____

_____ .

_____ .

By using the word "specialize" you will be forced to focus only on the key or core components of your company. The space I have left you is deliberately brief. This is to force you to pare down your answer.

Here is an example of one company's WWD statement:

> "Mr. Robertson, It's Bob Charendoff calling from Cybermation Inc. We specialize in automation software for MVS and distributed environments. Mr. Robertson, the reason for my call today is . . ."

Once you have established a WWD statement your next step is to test it in a role play situation. How does it sound? Does it flow into your next thought? Is it too long? Does it detract from your overall message. Play with it, edit it, revamp it.

One thing I like to recommend is to call existing customers and share the WWD statement with them. Get their impact and feedback. Get their perspective on what they think you do. You might be surprised at what they say. You might find they have a superb WWD statement that describes your company.

The last step is to incorporate the WWD statement and use it!

Section Five: Questions That Sell

29

Nine Steps to More Effective Questions

The key to successful questioning is, without a doubt, preparation and planning. Here are nine steps you can use as a reminder the next time you question.

1. Define Your Call Objective

This point cannot be hammered home enough. Without an objective, how can you determine the nature and the type of questions? Is the purpose to sell, generate a lead, make an appointment, inform, invite, or persuade?

2. Develop a Roadmap

Even the experts need a kickstart on the basics from time-to-time. I chuckled when noted telesales trainer, Art Sobczak, told me that he had hastily laid down the telephone receiver halfway through dialing on a sales call because he realized he wasn't totally prepared. Wisely he hung up and regrouped. Reaching your call destination requires a map or an outline. Determine the type of questions you need to ask to reach your objective.

3. Building a Bridge: Explain the Reason for Asking

Prospects tend to be a suspicious lot. They like to buy, but they sure hate to be sold; they are often wary of salespeople. Therefore, if you launch into your questioning mode the prospect might clam up. Explain your purpose. From a sales viewpoint you might ask:

> "Mr. Fisher, I would first like to ask you a few questions so I can determine if my product can specifically benefit you, okay?"

From a customer service point of view you might preface your questioning with,

"I can see you are upset Mrs. Fenton. In order to help you I would like to ask you a few questions."

4. Start with a Sigmund Freud Question

These are open-ended questions designed to get the customer talking. Imagine yourself as a doctor who is trying to diagnose a particular problem. From their response you can gauge their tone, evaluate their remarks, gather clues with regard to their personality, and collect other valuable data to help evaluate the situation.

5. Use Joe Friday Questions

Remember the TV series, Dragnet? Joe Friday wanted "just the facts." Close-ended questions help confirm and clarify facts. Use them carefully and in measured doses so as to prevent the customer from feeling that he/she is being interrogated.

6. Build Upon the Questions You Ask

You can reach almost any destination on a roadmap by several different routes. So, too, with questioning. Rookie and veteran sales reps often are too rigid in their questioning method. Be flexible. Be prepared to deviate from your outline when salient information is provided. However, be prepared to lead the conversation toward your destination if you find you have gone astray.

7. Take Notes as You Go

So much good information is lost simply because a sales rep forgets. As a general rule, most of us have poor memories. Even if you have exceptionally good listening skills (which you should), it is easy to confuse one customer with another, especially if the rep is making several presentations per hour. Taking notes forces you to listen to that particular customer. It is also a great way to collect data on things like common objections or complaints.

8. Use Silence

Ask your questions, and then SHUT UP! Your silence is not only courteous, but it also forces the customer to talk. Silence is a vacuum that begs to be filled. Let the customer "listen" himself into a sale.

9. Know When to Quit

This comes with time, experience, and a solid understanding of your product or service. There will come a moment when you "sense" you have the information to deliver your sales message or tackle the complaint. You will know you have gone too far when you experience those long, awkward silences as you struggle to find another question to ask.

Review this material once a day before you begin your calling. Evaluate yourself against these steps at the end of the day. How did you do? Questioning skills, like every other telesales skill, must constantly be honed to a sharp edge.

30

Scripting: The Question Aid

Job aids are tools used to help you achieve your call objective. The questioning job aid is designed to help you get the information you need to qualify or sell an account. Apart from assisting you in meeting your objective, the question aid will help your call flow more smoothly in less time.

Why Question?

Once a customer or prospect has shown interest in your opening statement, the next step is usually to ask questions. We ask questions for two reasons. First, it gets the customer involved in a meaningful dialogue. He/she becomes an integral part of the selling process and it is here where the "scripted"' format changes from rigid to flexible. Second, we ask questions to identify needs. The only way we can sell or qualify the prospect is to uncover motivators.

What to Do

Determine the key questions you must ask if you are to sell or qualify. Sometimes there are only a few questions; other times they are more extensive. Highlight questions that absolutely must be asked. Where possible, group them into a logical sequence and create defaults. For example, if a customer says "yes" to a question it may lead to a different set of questions than if the customer says "no."

Next, script an opening to your questioning. I call this a "questioning bridge." because it bridges the gap from the opening remarks to your questioning sequence. For example,

> "Ms. Taylor, in order to determine if this policy will fit your specific needs, I'd like to take a moment or two and ask you some questions. How does that sound?"

This tells the prospect what you are going to do and why. Typically, it helps open up the prospect.

Your first question should be open-ended in nature. The reason? So the prospect warms up. One opening line that has significant success is,

> "Tell me a little about your business (department, unit, company etc.)"

As simple and as broad as the question might seem, it works, and works well. It is a great opportunity to see where the prospect begins, how he frames the answer, what issue takes priority. You also get a feel for his type of personality as reflected in his voice and words. From there, the question you created in your job aid can be applied.

Of course you can narrow the focus of that first question:

> "Tell me how you go about processing a claim."

Or,

> "Tell me about your operating environment."

Warnings

> 1. Caution: customers don't always follow your scripting process. You, therefore, must be flexible in your questioning sequence. Don't become dependent upon it.

> 2. When using a questioning job aid there is a tendency to ask the question by rote and to not listen to the answers. You can miss a lot of important information by focusing on the trees and not the forest. Customers don't always oblige us with the anticipated answers; sometimes they are vague, sometimes they go off on tangents, sometimes they give us too much. Be prepared to dig.

> 3. Don't use too many consecutive closed-ended questions. After three consecutive questions pros-

pects get irritated; by five they are annoyed; at seven they are suspicious and angry. There are two reasons for this: first, they are not involved. Second, it feels like an interrogation. Learn to mix and match open- and closed-ended questions.

4. Limit questions when prospecting and generating leads. No more than seven or eight is a good rule. In scenarios where the prospect doesn't know you, your company, or your product, their patience factor is usually thin. So, determine which questions are critical in qualifying the status of a lead and use those first.

It is difficult to script a word-for-word questioning sequence in all but the simplest applications. The questions you develop should act only as a guide to achieve your objective. Keep the questions in front of you on a sheet and note the answers by writing them down.

31

Note Taking: Making Questioning More Effective

You know the importance of questioning. But all the questioning in the world won't amount to a hill of beans if you don't capture and retain the information that is supplied to you. This chapter focuses on the art of effective note taking,

Why Take Notes?

Notes are essential. Period. You can't remember even a fraction of what you hear.

Note taking also helps you focus on the clients' remarks and gives you a detailed roadmap of their needs, wants, and concerns. Additionally, note taking helps you build a history which will help you continue the story with your client on the next call.

Another point: note taking puts your client at ease by letting him or her know that you know what's going on. Nothing impresses a client more than your ability to keep tabs on his/her individual situation. Being able to recount events wields a good deal of persuasive power.

How to Take Notes

If you do take notes, chances are you use a sheet of paper or your computer screen and list the information as you hear it. This is fine, but the end result is often a confused mass of information in linear fashion with little or no regard for the logic or manner in which it should be classified. This usually means you have to flip-flop around to gather the data in order to use it to sell. Don't be surprised at this point. The mind does not always provide the information in a logical, neatly organized context—more often than not it is random.

Mind Mapping

You need a way to collect the information you receive in a manner that is conducive to making your presentation easier. Here's how: Start by taking a large sheet of paper (forget using your "notes" on the computer screen). I like 11" x 17" paper. Next, draw a circle in the middle. Then extend lines from the circle like rays from the sun. At the end of each line is a topic heading that you choose based on the type of products or services you sell. Prepare a list of questions that relate to these topics that you can use as a guide.

The diagram below is an example of a sales rep calling veterinarians regarding an insurance product.

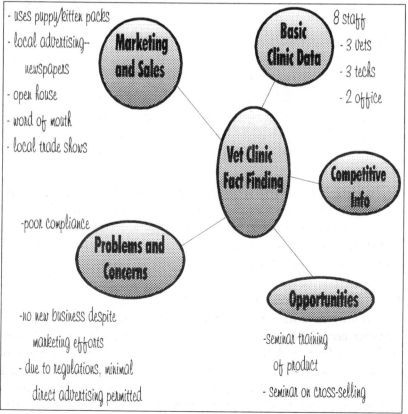

Mind mapping question example using an insurance product.

The rep uses the list of questions as a prompt, but, recognizing that customers provide data in their own manner, the caller is free to bounce among the key areas and quickly write in the responses. The end result looks like spaghetti but the information is logged where it should be. You can leave it like it is or transfer it elsewhere.

Benefits of Using this Method

As suggested, clients do not always provide information based on your questions. They bounce back and forth from topics depending on where their logic takes them. This method allows you to place the information in logical blocks, meaning easier and faster access and retrieval of data. It is also great when it comes to summarizing the clients' situation rather than leafing through reams of pages or burrowing through extensive notes. Another thing: It impresses the heck out of clients when you can collate remarks taken from a 5 or 10 minute interview. It shows you were not only listening but are capable of organizing the information. Finally, if you need to provide the client with follow up information, it is a superb way of saving time in searching through your notes.

Additional Resource

For more information on this topic, I suggest the book, *"Mindmapping: Your Personal Guide to Exploring Creativity & Problem Solving,"* by Joyce Wycoff, Berkley Books, New York.

32

The Psychology of Open-Ended Questions

We all know that in today's telesales environment one of the keys to selling and servicing lies in our ability to question effectively. And the best way to uncover needs or determine the cause of a customer complaint is through the use of open-ended questions. Unfortunately, we are not always mindful of the process of questioning. Here is another perspective to take with you the next time you are in the process of fact finding.

When you think of open ended questions, think of Sigmund Freud, a psychiatrist in the late 19th century in Vienna. He was a big proponent of psychotherapy. Instead of a frontal lobotomy or shock therapy, Sigmund felt it might be more effective to have the patient lie down on a couch and discuss his or her phobias, anxieties or whatever.

The Role of Facilitator

The role of psychoanalyst is that of a facilitator. He or she, prompts the patient to speak by using open-ended questions. For example, "How do you feel about that?" And, "What seems to be troubling you?"

The psychoanalyst then sits back. Slowly but surely the patient begins to discuss his or her anxieties and, hopefully, comes to some conclusions themselves.

Psychotherapy has since become the basis for things like career, marriage and student counseling. It means getting the individual to talk. In essence you should see yourself not so much as a salesperson, but rather as a sales "therapist." Your job is to help the customer uncover his/her own particular wants or needs. You must coax the information from them before you can prescribe any treatment.

When you are speaking with a customer, be it a sales call or an inquiry, picture them as a patient who has just entered your office via the telephone. Envision them lying on a couch beside your desk. See yourself with pen in hand poised above your notepad ready to take notes. Start your session with an open ended question like, "Ms. Fenton, how do you presently distribute your products?"

Why Open-Ended Questions?

Of course this type of question invites a more elaborate response than a close-ended question. There are four reasons why you should start off this way.

1. It gets the customers involved. It has often been said in sales that a customer should do 80% of the talking.

2. You understand the customer's want or need.

3. These questions are designed to help customers understand their own wants and needs. It is amazing how many customers will talk themselves into a sale when answering a question.

4. The customer knows that you want to help. This is vital. Buying is an emotional issue. People want to feel good about their purchase decision. Customers want to know that you are on their side; that you are willing to help them feel good. And sales therapy, like psychotherapy, is really nothing more than a discussion on emotions and feelings.

Customers often have hangups—call them phobias—about buying. For example, we know customers like to buy but they hate to be "sold." When they come to their own conclusions about the purchase decision they feel much better as opposed to having been "talked into the sale" by someone else.

In fact, one of the best types of questions you can use are the "feel" and "think" questions. Psychiatrists love them too because everyone has feelings and thoughts. For example, asking a customer,

"Tell me about the capabilities of your current supplier,"

might not provide all the information you desire because the customer might not know all the capabilities of the supplier.

However, if you asked

"Tell me how you feel about the capabilities of your current supplier," or,

"What do you think about their service warranty?",

invites an emotional response. In other words, you are asking for a opinion rather than a factual, objective analysis. Everyone has feelings, but not everyone has opinions.

Uncovers Hot Buttons

These type of questions are deeper than they appear. If we remember that buying is an emotional event, that people want to feel good about their purchase decisions no matter what the size or cost, then these type of questions beg to be asked. When customers reply to how they feel, you are getting information that is personal. The customers are telling you about their "hot" buttons, the things that makes them tick, what personally motivates them to buy. This will then give you the framework on which to make your presentation.

Seeing yourself as a sales therapist rather than a salesperson will make a difference in the way you sell and I guarantee it will mean better results.

33

Joe Friday's Art of Uncovering "Just the Facts"

D o you remember the old TV series Dragnet? If not, or if you are a little vague, here is a recap.

Sergeant Joe Friday carried a badge. He was a cop in Los Angeles. Friday is perhaps best noted for the rendering of the famous line: "Just the facts, ma'am, just the facts!" The sergeant was the consummate detective who stuck to cold, hard facts when solving a crime rather an assumptions and conjecture.

We can use Joe Friday as a model when discussing closed-ended questions. Most writers and salespeople feel that a closed-ended question is one that elicits a simple "yes" or "no" as a response. I disagree. A closed-ended question is one that gets specific information but does not necessarily invite the customer to articulate further. For example, "How many employees do you have?", invites only one response—the actual number. It does not invite further elaboration. It is merely a tidbit of information. It confirms or verifies but it does not provide anything more meaningful than a yes or a no.

The Pros

The real beauty of closed-ended questions is that they provide a sales rep with a "controlling" mechanism when fact finding. If we go back to Joe Friday, you may recall that he directed the conversation by utilizing questions that elicited "just the facts." When you have a long-winded customer, or one who has strayed from the topic, a few well-chosen closed-ended questions will help you to get back on track. If you are not sure of something the customer has uttered, rephrase it and ask if it is a correct interpretation. Their one-word response will help you gauge your understanding.

The Cons

Joe Friday may have been an excellent cop when it came to solving crimes but I suspect he would have made a lousy telesales rep. Joe had a rather clipped manner when it came to questioning. Let's face it, he was intimidating. The suspects or witnesses were rarely given the chance to elaborate because of his rapid fire approach to questioning. It was though they were being grilled by a cop in a damp and dingy room with a single bulb swaying overhead.

And that is the trouble with close-ended questions if they are overused by a sales rep. If the customer is barraged with a flurry of close-ended questions, they tend to get annoyed, defensive and perhaps even hostile simply because they feel they are being grilled. Studies have shown that after four consecutive close-ended questions, customers start to get annoyed. By six or seven they are annoyed and by ten they are usually hostile.

The Blend

In the preceding chapter we discussed open-ended questions with reference to Sigmund Freud. We learned that if we act as sales "therapists" we get the customer to open up and express themselves. This can be very good but it has its drawbacks. Customers can ramble on forever. They can give you reams of information: most which might be useless to your selling or servicing effort. Without controlling your use of open-ended questions with close-ended questions, you will stray from your call objective, frustrate yourself, increase your call length and ultimately fail in everything you do in life (just kidding).

The solution, of course, lies in your ability to blend the Joe Friday style with Sigmund Freud style.

Section Six: Persuasive Presentations

34

Scripting: The Feature-Advantage-Benefit Job Aid

O ne of the most effective scripting tools a telephone sales rep can possess is a "FAB" job aid or chart.

FAB stands for "features, advantages and benefits," and it is a superb way of crafting your offer or your message. It is easy to use, and, when presented properly, gives a clear, concise message to your client or prospect. This really means better sales results because it educates the customer while painting a clear picture of the product and its benefits in a non face-to-face medium.

The Chart

FAB sheets have been around for years, but, surprisingly, they are not used to any great degree. Take a look at my example on the next page.

To put your own chart together, scan your product literature and/or get a product expert into your call center and list every possible feature you can think of. Eventually you can reorganize the feature column so that the top five or ten features are listed first. This makes for fast, easy reference. Interestingly, you will find that most clients are never interested in more than four or five features.

The advantage describes what the feature does. While it may seem obvious to you, a feature's advantage is not always clear to the client. Advantages help educate your client while reducing confusion and clutter. Sometimes a single feature may have several advantages depending on the situation, such as in

FAB Chart

Feature	Advantage	Benefit
3 Pricing Options	Flexibility to choose the option that meets your needs	Fits any budgetary situation
Gold Plan	• $24.75 per month • $2,500 coverage per incident • accidental death coverage • boarding fees	• best value for your $ • greatest peace of mind coverage

the case of the Gold Plan (see chart). You might not want to recite all of the advantages but list them all as reminders.

Of course, benefits are what customers buy. Take time and list the benefits relative to each feature. Usually customers will not have more than two benefits that need fulfilling.

Verbal Bridges

The way to make your FAB work in an effective manner is to bridge the feature to the advantage and the advantage to the benefit. In the example below, the verbal bridges are indicated in italics and help make a smooth transition from one column to the next.

"Ms. Taylor, I would recommend the Gold Plan for your beagle *which means* you have $2500 coverage per accident or illness, but *what this really means* to you is greater peace of mind knowing that your pet has maximum protection."

Take the time to list various verbal bridges that link the

ideas. These should be "word-for-word" phrases.

Summary

FAB sheets are great educational tools for you and your customers. A FAB sheet should be dynamic *which means* that you should constantly update the information and play with the mix of words so that a clear, concise message is developed. They are also flexible. For instance, you can start with a benefit:

> "Ms. Taylor, one way to ensure your peace of mind is by purchasing the Gold Plan which gives you $2,500 coverage per accident or illness."

While it is a little awkward to use at first, practice will make them work. Go back to the basics and create FAB sheets and then use them.

Feature	Advantage	Benefit

Here's an example of a FAB sheet. Create one of your own, use your product or service, and list five features, then fill in with the advantages and benefits.

35

How to Increase Profits By Cross-Selling

Cross-selling is a superb way to increase the value of a sale by suggesting an accompanying product. When and where applicable, scripts should be developed for cross-selling opportunities. Developing a script for an add-on product is a combination of a word-for-word bridge and a job aid.

Take the Order First

There is one major rule to follow before attempting to use your cross-selling script: have the original order in hand. In other words, make sure you have achieved your primary objective first. Close the sale, take down the particulars, process the order and then, and only then, attempt the cross sell.

The Bridge

Once the order has been taken, then bridge to the cross sell item. For example,

> "Thank you Ms. Schroeder for the bubble jet printer order. Incidentally, did you know that we have ink jet cartridges on sale this month for 20% off? Not only will it save you some money but it will eliminate the hassle of running out and finding a cartridge when it needs replacing. Would you like me to add a couple of cartridges to the order?"

Note that the cross-sell relates directly to the purchase and that the item is relatively low-cost in comparison to the original order (therefore, a major purchase decision is not nec-

103

essary). From a scripting point of view, the item is a commodity and therefore needs little or no description. Secondly, by adding the word "incidentally" there is a casualness to the remark and reduces the "hard sell" feeling that sometimes accompanies an add-on sale. The benefits are clearly expressed and not belabored. Finally, there is a direct close.

The function of the job aid from a scripting perspective is to relate the purchased item to the add-on item. It is a quick reference source and reminder. For instance, look at the format of this job aid.

The Cross Selling Job Aid

Purchased Product	Add On Items	Benefits
Bubble Jet Printer	ink jet cartridges	• regular price: $20.00, on special for 20% off, save $2.00
	24 lb. laser quality paper	• buy 3 packages of 500 sheets and get the fourth free, save 25%

List the "Feature of the Month"

The job aid can be as simple as a sheet of paper, or can be added into the order processing software. For example, one company has installed a default to a job aid. Once the order has been entered into the computer and the "enter" button is touched, a pop-down screen appears listing the feature of the month, it looks something like this:

> ★ *Special Special* ★
>
> **"Oh, by the way, did you know we have the Norton Utilities package on sale this month for 30% off?"**

Tips for More Cross Selling

Before creating your cross sell script, do some homework. Examine the type of client to whom you will be selling. How knowledgeable are they? Will they see the add-on as a commodity, or something requiring a little more thought? Will they require additional information to make the purchase decision?

Answers to these questions will dictate the type of job aid you will require. In the above example for Norton Utilities, a Features-Advantages-Benefits sheet was developed that quickly explained the product to the customer who was not as familiar with the product and its use.

Be brief, to the point, and casual. Typically, no more than a line or two should be scripted. Try it for your next sale!

36

Use the "Primer Technique" for Cross- and Up-Selling

L et's talk about those situations when you're in an order-taking mode. You know, the phone rings, the friendly voice says, "Yes, I'd like to place an order." Regardless of whether these are the calls you handle all day long, or if they're a welcome respite from the grind of outbound calling, you can make these orders more valuable. And you can learn important selling skills in the process. I'm talking about cross-selling or up-selling. Specifically you can make the whole process easier on yourself by using the "primer" technique.

First of all, a cross-sell or an up-sell is easy because a sale has already been made. The customer is in a buying mood. What this really means is that he or she is open and positively inclined towards an additional purchase. A customer who has just bought can buy more. There are some who will argue that this is manipulative selling which takes advantage of a customer. I disagree. You are not being manipulative. In fact, you are being a *better* salesperson by reminding a customer of additional benefits that could be derived from the additional purchase. It's like when I go to McDonalds and the server says "Would you like fries with that today?" Something clicks inside and says "Yeah, sure. Sounds good."

Customers are intelligent people who make decisions every day. If they do not need or want the item that you have offered, they will tell you. There were times when I did not want fries with my Big Mac and I told the attendant that. Guess what? She neither leapt over the counter and knocked me down, nor was she the least bit offended. She offered it politely and I declined politely. So the message here is get rid of any hang-ups you might have about the customer perceiving you as some aggressive bully. You're not.

The Primer

"The Primer" is a technique that makes the process easier. The primer means that you have preconditioned or "primed" the customer for a cross- or up-sell. It goes like this,

Customer: "I would like to order the burgundy crewneck sweater, please."

Sales Rep: "Oh, that's a good choice."

Or, "I just love that one."

Or, "It's one of our most popular sweaters."

Or, "I think you will like that one."

Or, "I have one myself."

Of course, all these statements would have to be true if you were to use them. The point is that you are giving your approval of the customer's purchase decision. I know that must sound a little weird at first, but when most people buy an item, there is a moment of uncertainty. They wonder if they made the right choice, if they paid too much, or if they really needed it. Most of us consciously or unconsciously seek approval from others. By "approving" their purchase you actually make them feel "correct." In essence, they did the right thing.

The next step is easy:

Sales Rep: "You know, we have some great silk scarves that would go perfectly with that burgundy. Would you be interested?"

What's the very worst someone could say to you after you have just paid them a compliment about their original purchase decision? The worst one could say to you is "No, thank you."

But, more likely, you will have tremendous sales results.

Beyond Pre-Conditioning

Priming goes beyond pre-conditioning a customer to an additional purchase suggestion. It injects life, personality and charm into the conversation. Most of us are used to giving our orders to some bland, lackluster individual on the other end of the line. When we find someone who has an obvious interest in the product, we feel even more inclined to buy more. Enthusiasm is a catchy thing and adds a whole new element to the selling process.

To reemphasize, the comments on a particular product or service must be absolutely sincere. The majority of customers will know if you are scamming them. Cross-selling and up-selling is simply rich in potential.

37

10 Tips for Profitable Cross- and Up-Selling

Here are 10 tips to help you cross-sell and up-sell.

1. Sell First and Tell Later

Never, ever attempt to up-sell or cross-sell until you have all the information necessary to fulfill the first order. In our rush or excitement to up-sell we sometimes forget that the customer has an order to place. Selling additional items too early in the call might turn the customer off. You could lose the original sale.

2. The Rule of "25."

The value of an add-on sale should not increase the overall order by more than 25%. For example, if the original order is $100.00, you should be cautious in your attempts to exceed that order by $25.00. Despite the fact that people are motivated to buy, they still have a mental limit as to the amount they will dispense. For whatever reason, that figure rarely exceeds 25%. Generally, going above that value is only marginally successful.

3. Make a Profit

This is more of a management, rather than a salesperson decision, but the whole point of the exercise is to make money. The item(s) you choose must make enough profit to at least cover the cost of the additional time you spend on the phone. One source I've read claims that you must show at least a $4.00 profit on each add-on sale.

4. Don't Dump Junk

There is, on occasion, the urge to use cross-selling and up-selling to move unwanted inventory. This in itself is okay provided the customer isn't saddled with useless or defective products. If you are clearing stock that won't be replaced, let the customer know. If it is a discontinued line, don't hesitate in letting the customer know. If you don't, you'll be sorry later.

5. Limit and Relate

Limit your choice of add-on items to those that clearly relate to the original purchase. If a customer were buying a blazer he has seen in a catalogue, suggesting a shirt and a tie makes sense. Suggesting a goose-necked garden hoe, however, does not.

6. Familiarity Breeds Success

The more familiar your customer is with the add-on item, the more likely he or she is to buy. Cross-selling and up-selling is not the time to introduce a brand new product, unless the price is unusually low (Refer to #3.) New products take time to sell using features and benefits. This will take additional time. The purpose of the up-sell is to increase the order while the buying motive is strong. Introducing something unfamiliar will only confuse the customer.

7. Plan, Plan, Plan and Plan Again

Again, likely a management issue, but your life will be much easier if the program is well planned and implemented. For instance, not only must you decide which products to sell, you must determine what product(s) they relate to. So, if you are going to up-sell with ties, you've got to decide, in advance, which blazers they will match.

8. Train to Avoid Pain

Ensure that you are trained on the products or services offered. Make sure you understand them. Rehearse the skills necessary to get the customer to say "yes." One catalogue firm spends 40 hours on training designed to demonstrate how a particular add-on applies to and benefits the customer.

9. Test with the Best, then Roll With the Rest

Okay, another management issue that you might want to make your manager aware of. Test your cross-selling and up-selling with your best people. They have the drive and initiative to work out any of the kinks. Introduce the cross-selling and up-selling program to the rest of the sales reps only after you are sure of the test results.

10. E=MC2

Your cross selling efforts (E) will be directly dependent on how motivated (M) you are. Cross-selling and up-selling takes additional time and effort. If there is no reward . . . if you are not motivated . . . chances are the program will not be a rip roaring success. Compensation (C) is always a critical factor in selling and perhaps more so when you are asking for that little extra with each sale. The other "C" stands for Control. Whether you are a sales rep or a manager, the ability to control the direction of the cross-selling and up-selling activities will determine success. In other words, measure your productivity, your performance and your profitability. If there is something lacking in any one of these areas, make changes.

Section Seven: Closing for Commitment

38

Scripting: The Importance of The Close

The close in the sale can and should be scripted. The reason is that the close is the final "action" item on your script. It is what you want the prospect or the customer to do and therefore is the most critical component. If you do not fully script the close, there is a good chance it will not get done.

Script your close word-for-word. When you have taken the time to craft a clear, concise close, there is no misinterpretation by the customer or the prospect. Word-for-word scripting ensures that the message is not vague or uncertain.

Tips

1. Summarize Your Findings

> "Ms. Parris, if I understand you correctly, you are looking for a medium-priced bubble jet or ink jet printer. You'll use it primarily for word processing and spread sheets but graphics are not a key concern. Speed of printing is not a major issue, but you might be looking at color copies down the line . . ."

This indicates to the customer that you were listening and that you understand their needs. The summary is directly related to the questions that you had developed earlier in your script.

2. Preface Your Close

One of the most effective prefaces is,

> "Ms. Parris, based on all that you have told me, I would like to recommend *(insert your solution, product offering etc.)*"

This scripted phrase does two things. First, it offers a recommendation. Second, by stating you have a "recommendation" customers and prospects listen further. Buyers like "recommendations." It is non-threatening, and consultative in nature. Also, subtly, it prepares the customer for the close.

3. Script Your Close

Go back to your pre-call planning. What was the objective of the call? The objective determines your close. If the objective was to sell, then prepare a direct or assumptive close. If the objective was to sell a printer, then the close might look like this,

> "I would like to recommend the PH Ink Jet 900. It meets all your requirements and your investment is only $429.00. Now, I can have that couriered today and in your office by tomorrow morning. All I need is a credit card or a purchase order number to get you started."

4. Script the Words, "SHUT UP!"

Of course, these words are to act as a reminder that you have made an assumptive close and that the decision now rests with your prospect. I find that if I don't add this reminder into the script, that inevitably the sales rep continues to blurt out additional information which can ultimately result in the loss of the sale.

5. Prepare Fallback Scripts for Secondary Objectives

In the previous example, the prospect may legitimately ask for something in the mail or by fax (a brochure, a spec sheet etc.) While you should treat this as an objection and utilize your objections job aid, you should also be prepared to fulfill the prospect's request. If you have qualified the request for the literature make certain you script a follow-up close. For example,

> "I will *(fax/send/courier)* that information to you by *(date/time)*. Let's arrange to discuss it further. How does tomorrow morning at *(indicate specific time)* look for you?"

This close creates action and commitment. On the one hand, the prospect must look at his/her calendar to set the appointment. On the other hand, it implies that he or she must read the documentation.

Summary

Scripting the close is no different from any other element of the scripting process. It simply involves analyzing the objective and determining the likely responses of the customer. The only real difference in the close is its importance. Because it is designed to move the customer to commit or respond or buy or whatever, it is critical. Take the time to script and practice your closes.

39

Close Early and Often, or Wait a While?

Too often sales reps, supervisors and their managers labor under the impression that telesales is a "one step" process. In other words, you make a call and you either sell or you don't. Closing on a single call can be a mistake, and, in fact, there are times when a second or third call should be made before you ask for the sale. Here's a look at using separate and distinct call strategies to close the sale.

Two Main Points

First, customers/prospects don't always adhere to your schedule. They often need time to think, assimilate, and check out other options. In short, there are times when closing just doesn't make sense from the client's perspective. Attempting to do so could harm the sale.

Second, you can not always assimilate the data you have received to make a reasonable proposal. You might well need the time to gather the information and formulate a proposal for the next call.

Strategically, there are some benefits to closing the sale on the second or third call. First giving the customer time to evaluate your presentation positions you as "longer term" in your relationship. You are not rushing the client and many will respect that. On the other hand some might argue that this allows the "fish to escape from the net." This is why you must carefully consider the type of product you are selling, the type of client you have on the phone, the sense of urgency, the competitive situation, and whether this is a one-time sale or the start of a long-run relationship.

Giving the Client Time to Ponder

If the product is complex and/or pricey, if the customer is analytical, if the competitive situation is tight and you are looking for multiple sales, the following technique might be used.

> "Mr. Burla, I recognize that this decision will require some thought. What I would like to do is give you a day to consider the proposal. I will call you tomorrow at 3:15 and we can discuss any other concerns you might have. If everything looks good, we can proceed with the sale. How does that sound?"

In this example, you have shown professional courtesy by allowing the time for contemplation. At the same time you are creating action by giving the client a specified time frame in which to mull over the proposal. As well, you are "closing" on the precise time of your next call. If the customer commits to the time, chances are that he or she will review your proposal with the view to buy.

Give Yourself the Time to Ponder

Another instance where you might wish to delay asking for the sale is after the initial questioning phase. As mentioned, you cannot always assimilate the detail provided. It is a great opportunity for sober thought of your own. So instead of forcing a presentation, and fumbling through a proposal or close, you might want to say,

> "Ms. Clemens, you have given me a lot of good information. What I'd like to do is take a day to go over the information and come back to you with a detailed proposal. I'd like to set up a telephone appointment for say, 30 minutes, tomorrow at 3:45. How does that sound?"

From your client's perspective, this strategy positions you as a thoughtful, consultative sales rep who does not have pat solutions or answers. It lends a certain amount of importance and value to the information you have received. Most clients will recognize and accept this. When you do make that return call with the proposal, use the opportunity to its fullest advantage. In other words, you have been given the time to review the information, so use the time to develop a good proposal.

Tips

Here are some tips. Before calling the client back, review the notes taken from your questioning "mind map" (see page 91). Collect the data and place them into the following categories: Current Situation and Solutions and Recommendations.

Under "Current Situation," summarize the customer's wants, needs, problems or concerns. Use the opportunity to verify and confirm that these issues are core to the client. Under "Solutions and Recommendations" list how your product or service can solve these wants, needs, problems or concerns. In other words, use features, advantages and benefits.

When you call, start the conversation with something like this:

> "Ms Clemens, as you know, I have taken the time to review my notes and I have come up with some ideas and solutions that might benefit you. What I would like to do is simply review your current situation to ensure that I have understood you correctly and then present some solutions. How does that sound?"

In this example, you are reminding the client that you took the time to give their situation individual attention. In addition, you are presenting a clear agenda of what you would like to do. It also shows what a tremendous listener you are. Again, this is consultative. The client feels that he or she is part of the process.

In conclusion, closing the sale a call or two later has some strategic benefits. It is not necessarily the wisest strategy in every situation, but there are times when it can and should be used. Consider your products/services carefully. Consider the individual client (decision maker) and his or her "buying style." Consider the future you would like to have with these clients. Consider, too, the type of image, you'd like to portray to these clients. Take time to consider the benefits.

40

And Here's the Pitch!

Here is a closing technique that has been successful for many sales reps I have taught. It is called the Pitch.

The Pitch is based on the simple premise that you know you are going to close, and that your customer knows you are going to close. So why not prepare them to receive the pitch?

Much like a batter who is awaiting a pitch, the customer is more or less waiting for the same thing. My recommendation is that you give him or her a verbal "wind up" so they are prepared for the pitch. This way the customer is not caught off-guard. In fact, he is looking down the pipe for the pitch.

It works like this.

> "Okay Mr. Martin, here's my pitch: You explained that you are looking for a software package that can quickly and thoroughly create a business and marketing plan. The Biz Pro Planner provides you a series of easy-to-use templates covering every topic from the executive overview, to mission statements, to target markets, situational analysis, budgets and everything in between. Not only do you have an outline of topics, but also a series of prompts that give you tips and ideas on how to proceed. What this really means is you not only save time but you have the peace of mind that you have produced a comprehensive plan for your customers. So there's the pitch. Shall I write up the order?"

Note: Like a pitcher on the mound, I went into my routine so that the batter knows the ball is about to be thrown. In this case, my routine or windup is a summary of the customer needs and a few features and benefits. The final delivery is the request for the order.

For most reps, there is a degree of anxiety at the moment of closing. The anxiety stems from a variety of reasons, not the least of which is the fear that you are being a bit too bold and presumptuous by asking for the sale. Using the pitch helps relieve the anxiety. It is a casual no-nonsense method of letting the customer know what is coming up next.

The close sometimes catches the customer off-guard. They are not prepared for it and many are left momentarily uncertain or confused. If customers know they are about to be pitched, they are not caught unprepared, and they are more apt to focus on your summary and close. This, of course, is the precise time you want the customer to be listening.

41

Sure Ways to Lose a Sale

A great way to lose a sale is to ignore—or forget to mention—the little nitty-gritty details when closing the sale.

A case in point was a call I received from a telephone rep who had first sent me an intriguing letter about reprinting some articles I wrote for various magazines. These articles would be attractively laid out and printed on high-quality paper, featuring the magazine's name. I felt these could be used as a great marketing tool. The follow-up call came within three days. Good so far.

The sales rep did the fact finding, handled my objections with some innovative work, then laid out the price with tax and closed the sale. Super performance! To verify everything, I was asked to send a fax outlining which articles, agreement on the quantities and on the price. This I did. (She began slipping here, as she should have recapped everything and faxed it rather than leaving me with the grunt work.)

About three or four weeks later, I received a voice message from the rep. She explained that she had everything ready to go but had not yet received a check for one-half the payment. Nothing had been done.

No where in any conversation—letter or fax—was that little detail mentioned.

I could have called back. But I didn't. It had lost its sense of urgency and importance after three weeks.

LESSON: Don't blow the sale because of the little stuff.

And finally, another way to lose a sale is to neglect making a couple more follow-up calls. In the previous example the sales rep had a 50/50 chance of rekindling my interest if she could deal with the check. Instead, she relied on a single voice mail message and, I guess, she assumed I had lost interest. She will never know unless she reads this book.

LESSON: Be aggressive and follow-up your calls.

Losing a sale before the sale has been made is dreadful (but understandable). But losing the sale after the sale has been made is abominable (and unforgivable). Once you have a fish on the line, don't let your line go slack until the fish is in the boat.

42

Give Full Disclosure During Your Calls

By now you should be well aware that when you open a call you should state your name, the company you represent, and the reason and benefit of your call. Great. Assuming everything goes according to plan on the call, you'll need to end it effectively to sew up the details.

I suggest "full disclosure" at the call's end, and it applies whenever a sale is made, whether it be inbound or outbound. Full disclosure is simple. It is nothing more than giving the customer the bottom line.

It goes something like,

> "Okay, Ms. Muirhead, just to make sure everything is correct, you want five units, right? The cost of each unit is $20.00, so your total price is $100.00. Now with tax and shipping your total price is $115.85."

Let's take a look at that full disclosure. It should be done routinely. Stating the total price is not always mentioned but a good sales rep will do so. But the clincher, in my opinion, is having the guts and the professionalism to mention those sundry extra charges like tax and shipping.

I know that many teleprofessionals would—and do—shy away from mentioning the extra charges that are typically tagged on to a purchase. Most reps justify their behavior by stating that the purchaser "expects" these charges, that they are a part of doing business. Maybe so, but they often come as a nasty surprise to most customers. Customers have a neat way of forgetting about those charges. And customers also have a way of getting annoyed with the company and the sales rep when the price is suddenly 16% higher than they had originally thought.

Most customers will suffer through this little indignation and, despite being burned, they will likely buy again, all things being equal. But if you are personally interested in being a total professional and if you want to differeniate yourself from the rest of the pack, then practice full disclosure.

43

A Simple, But Effective Close

Here's the story of a great call I received. From start to finish, this rep knew his stuff. He was well prepared, his tone was friendly, the opening statement provocative, his fact finding and presenting skills were superb. But what really impressed me was his closing technique. It went like this.

> "So, Mr. Domanski, why not give it a try? And, if you are not satisfied you can give me a call and I will personally handle your full refund. Do you have a pen and paper handy? *(pause)* My name again is Richard Maisoneuve. M-A-I-S-O-N-E-U-V-E. And my phone number is xxx-xxxx. Now, just to verify, your address is . . . ?"

Let's take a look at this remarkable close. First of all, Richard suggested giving it a "try." It is a well known fact that most purchasers suffer a little doubt when they buy. They may wonder if they made the right decision, if their neighbors, etc., will approve, if the product will work. To some degree, this rep alleviated that fear. He instilled in my mind the belief that, at worst, the purchase was a "trial." I could always argue with myself that I was not stuck with a raw deal. I liked that. He got me to convince myself.

Eliminated an Objection in Advance

Richard cemented the deal by promising a full refund if I was not delighted. He eliminated the objection before I could think to raise it. There can be little doubt that an iron clad guarantee can sway the minds of many a doubtful decision maker. Unfortunately, not all products come with a full guarantee and warranties to see how they apply. Some have limitations and you should be aware of these before you use them.

But the guarantee wasn't the clincher. Oh, I admit, it played a role in my decision to buy. However, what really convinced me to give this product a try was Richard's "personal guarantee." Richard got me going by urging me to find a piece of paper and a pen. He waited until I confirmed I had the items in hand. And then he proceeded to give me his name and took the time to spell it. Slowly. Followed by the phone number.

Giving your full name and number is making yourself accountable. That's powerful stuff in my mind. Because, Richard was giving me somewhere to go if something screwed up. I could find him. Track him down if need be. He could not hide. He was saying that his role did not end with the taking of an order. And never, ever before has a telesales rep given me his name and number in that manner.

Builds Confidence

There is another element at work here. I believed him. I believed him not because of the actual words he used but rather how Richard sounded when he said them. They were delivered with easy confidence. Not cockiness; confidence. It was the voice of someone who truly believed in the product. It was the voice of someone who knew that in all likelihood there would not be a problem, but if there was, he would gladly step in.

When I sat down to do this chapter I was inspired by how simple Richard's approach was to his close. But as I write these words, I am struck by the richness of thought that went into the development of his script. My hat is off to Richard.

But Wait, There's More: The Follow-Up

That's not the end of the story. Richard called again. And once again, he did not disappoint. His follow-up technique was nothing short of superb. Here's what happened.

Richard called and identified himself, his company, and then reminded me of his call a few weeks earlier. He went on to explain that he was calling to make certain that I was totally satisfied with my purchase. Richard then went on to ask me a series of questions. He inquired about the delivery. Was it on time, well packaged? Did the product meet my expectations? Were there any questions about the product, its usage, or the warranty? Any concerns? I was extremely pleased with the product and with Richard. At this point he said,

> "You know Mr. Domanski, I came across an article that might interest you on household hints. It's about using environmentally friendly products to clean your home. These are good tips and most households have all the ingredients necessary to make the cleaning solutions so it will save you some money. Can I send it to you along with a catalogue of some of our other household products?"

Gee, how could you say no to an offer that was free and designed to save me money? Let's take a look at this follow-up call.

The Three Steps

Richard executed all the basic steps correctly. He,

1. Identified himself,

2a. Identified his company,

2b. Established rapport (reminded me when and why he called), and,

3. Stated the reason for the call.

But Richard added another ingredient to his follow-up call which I have rarely seen. He added value. The fact that he called to determine my satisfaction was impressive in itself. But by offering to send me an article which was designed to save me money with products that were environmentally friendly and with no strings attached . . . that went well beyond what most telesales reps bother to do.

And then he, oh, so subtly, got me to accept a catalogue of their additional products.

Now you tell me, when the catalogue and article arrives in

the hefty stack of mail I receive daily, which do you think will be read first? Do you think I will be favorably inclined to buy additional products in the future?

Richard has obviously been trained well. Whoever it was that trained him must have explained that a follow-up call should always carry some added value for the customer. The instructor must have told Richard that it doesn't matter if you have known the customer for two days or two years. Each call must provide some measure of value. If nothing else, adding value in little ways will differentiate your company and products from those of your competitors.

Creating Value

Making a follow-up call with value is not always easy work. One of the best ways to approach this task is start to build up a library of articles, clippings and the like that you can send when appropriate. And they don't have to necessarily relate to your product (but it makes good sense to demonstrate the additional value of your product, if you can.)

For example, I purchased a time management system at quite some cost well over a year ago on behalf of myself and the group I worked with. The sales rep has since called me to let me know of new additions and modifications. Every call has been supplemented with an article on time management or goal setting techniques.

But the material you send does not have to be related to your business or industry. I have another individual who will send me jokes or cartoons on a fairly regular basis. I look forward to them. Every one of them brings a smile to my face and that, too, is value for certain types of customer. Make sure the material you send goes beyond company literature. There is a time and a place for brochures and flyers: when you are selling. But they are not usually value-added.

The point is, you must do a little more. You have to find an edge and keep it finally honed. Richard Maisoneuve has obviously understood the concept when it comes to follow-up calls. Learn from Richard.

Section Eight: Turning Around Objections

44

Scripting: The Objections Job Aid

An objections job aid is relatively simple to craft and should be an integral part of your script. It's a chart that consists of three parts: objection, bridge, and response/probe.

You can anticipate about 98% of the objections you'll encounter if you take the time to think as a customer or prospect.

Do it.

Sit down and divide the objections into four broad categories: Price, Product, Postponement and Personal. Create a chart(s) for each category for fast and easy reference during your calls.

Under price, for example, list all the possible objections that relate to budgets, terms, financing, discounts etc. Under product, list every conceivable product objection. Postponement refers to "brush off" objections such as "I would like to think about it," or "Send me something in the mail." Finally, personal objections refer to gripes or complaints the client has with you personally (hopefully not) or your company.

Your chart should contain a section for a "bridge." A bridge is simply a technique or method for showing sympathy to your client's objection. For example, "I understand," or "That is a good point," are two bridges that indicate you are listening (but not necessarily that you agree).

The third element is the direct response or probe to that particular objection. You can develop these responses ahead of time and eventually add to or edit them accordingly once you have gained more experience.

The objections chart should be updated and changed as frequently as required. Use heavier stock paper and/or color

Section Nine: Profitable Telesales Strategies

50

Making the Most of Every Call: Gather Information

There is a way to maximize and leverage every call you make regardless of whether or not a sale is made: See every call as an opportunity to formally gather information that can be used to market more effectively in the future.

I call this gathering "market intelligence." And in today's fast paced competitive environment, getting a quick pulse of the marketplace can mean the difference between success and failure.

What it Is and Isn't

Market intelligence is the formal process of gathering information about virtually any topic by using a questionnaire format. Don't confuse this with market research. Market research implies scientific controls for gathering information, analyzing it and applying it in some strategic manner. Market intelligence, on the other hand, is a means of quickly discerning trends, ideas, concerns, market identification, opportunities, threats and weaknesses among other things.

It must be used with caution because the information will only give you a "feel" of the marketplace. However, in the absence of time and budget for very formal and lengthy market surveys, market intelligence can work quickly and easily. Here's how to go about setting up a market intelligence program.

1. Define Your Objectives

What do you want to learn? Stay focused. Remember one

thing: You can ask anything you want. You just can't ask *everything*. Again, stay focused! If you want to understand more about price, focus on price. If you want to learn about your competitor determine precisely what you want to know. Delivery? Terms? Don't try to do it all.

2. Create Your Survey

Objectives in hand, develop your questions. Some key points: Just like lead generation questions, the maximum number of questions should not exceed seven or eight. Beyond that point the prospect gets antsy and the quality of the information begins to dilute rapidly. Time is critical and the questions should not take any more than a minute or two to complete. Incidentally, you don't necessarily have to craft six or seven questions. If two or three questions suffice, use them. Don't abuse the opportunity. Your questions must be short and to the point. Too many open-ended questions are hard to record accurately so they must be balanced carefully. On the other hand, too many closed-ended questions can not only annoy your prospect but limit the effectiveness of your questions. Have forms made up beforehand so that you can quickly complete them. This makes the information more accurate and easier to compile.

3. Who Should You Ask?

You can gather your market intelligence from anyone. You can survey existing clients or you can survey prospects. You can survey those who have just purchased—from either you or a competitor. Or those who have simply said no.

4. When Should You Ask?

While you can have a specific campaign to gather market intelligence the real opportunity lies with asking your questions at the conclusion of any call. Make sure you have completed your original call objectives first before you launch into your survey.

5. Script Your Request

The key to gathering market intelligence is to ask. And how you ask is vital. Not unlike an opening statement of a cold call, the request for information should be tied to a benefit. Here's an example of a request from a customer who has just purchased from a competitor:

> "Mr. Anderson, I very much respect your decision to purchase from ABC Co. Before I go, I was wondering if I could take about a minute more of your time and ask you three or four questions? We are always trying to improve our product offering and we have found that asking questions of prospects who purchase from a competitor gives us tremendous insights. As a result we have made some changes that really benefit customers. Do you have moment?"

Based on my experience, 98% of prospects agree. Two factors affect this. First, most of them feel a little badly when they announce they have gone to a competitor. Secondly, there is the implied benefit of an improved product down the line. On a larger level, you position your company in a favorable light by showing no hard feelings and by trying to learn from the event.

6. How Many?

The number of surveys you take is vital. Too few and the integrity of your findings will be compromised. Too many and the effort becomes bulky and difficult to assess (in which case you should be doing "market research.") A good rule of thumb is to make at least 100 surveys and probably no more than 200 maximum. This will give you a decent sampling of the market and provides you with some confidence level in the decisions you make.

7. Acknowledge /Thanks

Thank the prospect/client. While it can be a little difficult and time consuming to manage, it is a good idea to send a little thank you card to the participants. Apart from being courteous, it keeps the door open for future surveys.

8. Compile and Analyze

Compile the results and refer to your objectives. Look for trends and other indicators. Look for opportunities. Don't be afraid to make a few follow-up calls if you want a prospect/

client to elaborate on a specific point. (But don't abuse the privilege.) Be strategic.

9. Act!

Knowledge is not power. Knowledge is only potential power. Use the information you have. Act on it. But bear in mind, market intelligence does not replace the formal process of market research.

51

How to Create Reasonable Doubt About Your Competition

To be truly effective and successful in telephone sales, you need to master the ability to create "reasonable doubt." Doubt that the competitor's product is the right choice. You do this by building and strengthening your knowledge on competitive products.

How and why does this work?

First, knowing your competitor's product/services will help you sell more. With competitive knowledge you can leverage their weaknesses and deflect their strengths. Secondly, you become more consultative with the prospect. By educating them about your product and your competitor's product, you show your professional expertise. You bring value, which prospects and customers appreciate.

How to Build Your Competitive Expertise

The first step is gathering information. Start with an analysis of your prospect. If you sell to a consumer, call from your home and ask for info to be sent to you. Collect every piece of marketing and promotional literature they're willing to send you.

Do the same thing if you sell to a business. Start by calling the competitor and request the information be sent directly to your company address. You will be amazed at how many will do so. Requests for literature are so frequent, most people filling the requests don't pay attention, or aren't trained to look for competitors. If that doesn't work, have a friend who works at another business call the competitor and request information.

If you're still coming up empty, position yourself as an independent consultant, researcher or agent and request the information be sent to your home. Give yourself a company name.

Analysis

The next step is to analyze the material you receive. You can do this in a workshop format with other sales reps or managers, or even on your own.

Read the literature carefully. Assess the look and presentation. How are they positioning their product or service? High end, low end, in between? Where is your material positioned? Are you dealing head to head? To whom is the piece targeted: end user, decision maker, influencer, or all three? How does that compare to your efforts?

What are the key selling features and benefits? How do they compare to your material? Can you discern their "unique selling proposition" (USP), the one thing that they are trying to hammer home? For instance, is it price? Value? Service? Quality?

Analyze the cover letter if there is one. What does it tell you about the company? Big, formal, conservative or smaller and friendlier? Or just blah?

Now, using this information determine if you are going head-to-head. How do you differ? Can you find strengths in your product/service relative to your competitor's? How about weaknesses? Can you leverage these?

Quotes and Proposals

Learning about your competitor involves more than just reading promotional literature. Much of what a competitor has to say comes from a price quote or a proposal. Getting a copy of a competitor's proposal is not always easy. But I am forever amazed at how many reps won't even bother to ask. In situations where there is a competitive proposal or quote on the prospect's desk, try asking for it.

> "Ms. Pick, would it be possible for me to review
> ABC Company's proposal? The reason I ask is that
> I would like to ensure that we have an "apples to
> apples" comparison. This will save you a lot of time
> and effort trying to analyze and compare. How
> does that sound?"

Note that a request has been made with an explanation
which is tied to a benefit statement. Some prospects are only
too glad to have someone "assist" them in the decision making
process.

The third step in dealing with a competitive situation is to
create doubt in the mind of the prospect with regard to the
product/service. Here is an obvious truism: Don't slam the competition.

Regardless of the superiority of your product/service, don't
dump on the competition. (At least not directly.) Dumping of
the competition is petty. It sounds cheap and positions you as
unprofessional and somehow incapable of selling your product
on its own merit.

You create doubt with subtlety:

> "Have you inquired about the warranty? My un-
> derstanding is that it is limited to only ten days?"

In this example, the rep had learned the warranty was significantly different than his. The remark was designed simply
to create doubt in the mind of the client. It won't necessarily
guarantee the sale. And note the delivery: Polite, direct, and
very subtle. The rep added one more remark.

> "Mr. Martin, I am not certain, but I do not think
> their price includes shipping and handling while
> ours does. If you take that into account, there is
> only a marginal difference."

In this example, the rep suggests that he is "uncertain."
The idea was not to slash away but rather to delicately insert
the blade.

By the way, the rep got the sale. Whether it was entirely
due to these two remarks is not certain. There are many factors which impact the sale, however, creating the doubt in the
client's mind was likely a significant one.

54

When Sending Mail Is Worthwhile

Mailings to prospects and/or customers can be time consuming, expensive, possibly annoying to the recipient, and wasteful. Before you pop something in the mail, analyze why. Here are some circumstances where mailing is worth the effort.

1. Mail first when you are introducing telephone sales for the first time. If you're just beginning servicing them by phone, an introductory letter that highlights the benefits, preps the prospect, and paves the way for the call.

2. Send a letter when taking over an account from field sales. In some circumstances the customer might feel a sense of hostility for a perceived lack of service. Outline the benefits and rationale.

3. When you've replaced an existing inside rep. Loyalties are often created and the customer must learn to be loyal to you.

4. If you or your company has screwed up. Send a letter or note explaining what has happened and what is being done to rectify the problem. This tactic will help take a little (not all) of the sting out of your next call.

5. When you are introducing a new product/service to a new market. Note the word "new." Your targets do not know you, your company or your products. It's a frame of reference. But don't feel you always need to send a brochure on a new product to your existing base. They know you and your company. Before filling their in-basket with unwanted clutter, make sure there is interest.

6. Any product that is particularly complex. The brochure might act as a guide for your questioning and selling. It is a tangible piece of evidence. (A testimonial or two will work wonders here.)

7. If there is a risk factor involved with the purchase. Say you have a product that must meet certain standards or codes and the prospect or customer must be made aware of these stipulations. In this case, the written word is a good way to ensure compliance.

8. When your market matures. For example, suppose you and all your competitors are using the same strategy of calling the customer first and then mailing. This might be annoying or just plain boring. Use mail to differentiate yourself from the competitors.

9. When a calling strategy alone does not seem to be getting the results. First make certain your target is well defined, that your script is not at fault, and that the offer is a good one. If these elements are in check, then perhaps your market needs another approach. It can't hurt to test the mailing concept.

10. If you have a product that is not quite ready for distribution and you want to tease your target market with an advance notice. This also works to get the jump on your competition.

In summary, think before you mail. Mailing indiscriminately can be useless, wasteful and dangerous.

55

How to Increase Your Production Every Day

I am sure that you have noticed that not all calling times are created equal. There are peak hours to reach prospects and customers, and there are non-peak hours.

Peak hours are priority hours. Once you have determined what those hours are, you have the information you need to plan your day. Peak hours should mean only one thing to you: **CALLING**.

This is the time that you want to pick up the phone and begin dialing. You want to get on a roll, or into a groove and keep the momentum flowing. This is the time where you meet and exceed your objectives.

Logical in Theory More Than in Practice

As logical as this sounds, many sales reps squander the time needlessly. I've watched sales reps compose follow-up letters, stuff promotional literature, update their customer data, visit the fax machine, decide to take an R & R break, and otherwise squander away the best hours of the day.

Obviously, non-peak hours are least productive. For example, 8:00 a.m. to 9:00 a.m., lunch hours and late afternoons are typically poor calling times for many industries (but not all!). It is during these periods that you should be working on the housekeeping details.

Identify Your Peak Times

First, determine your peak and non-peak hours.

Next, force yourself to start calling during the peak hours, avoiding all other distractions. Keep a list of the follow-up items that need completing during non-peak periods. Or have an ACTION tray and for every item you must complete, throw it into the tray and work your way through it at appropriate times. Or, if you are computerized, utilize your notebook or "to do" file.

> **Quick Tip:** date each piece of paper or memo so you know when you began the task, and for every time you look at or handle that memo or paper, jot down a "/" or other tick mark to show how many times you handled it without acting on it. It's a great way to rid you of procrastination.

When an urgent matter arises during a peak period, ask yourself a question: What will happen if I do not complete this task right now, and why? If the consequences are grave, then obviously you must respond. If not, assign the task to a more appropriate time.

Give the Task Away

Delegating is not a luxury that everyone has. However, if there is some sort of support group, use it. Delegate the task of faxing, have someone else stuff envelopes, get someone else to do the photocopying, etc.

The trouble is, most of us like the opportunity to break the routine of calling, regardless of the time. *Avoid that trap at all costs.* It is addictive and eventually you will convince yourself that the task at hand must absolutely, positively be done at that very moment. Pause before starting a task during your peak hours and ask yourself if it is worth the effort now.

If you stick to these principles you will find your results will improve significantly.

56

Skills Don't Matter When the Strategy is Faulty

This is not a chapter on skills. It will demonstrate how good telesales skills can be submarined by lack of commitment from other departments within your company. Without this commitment, all the skills you have will not amount to much. Here's what happened to me.

This past winter I responded to a direct mail piece asking if I was interested in interlocking brick paving stones. Shortly after I sent the reply card, I received a call from Sandy, the telephone sales rep. Sandy had two objectives: to qualify me, and then to arrange an appointment. Good stuff so far. Score one point.

I asked Sandy to give me a call in late April, after the snow was gone (hopefully) and after my vacation. Sure enough, I received a call two days after my return. Score another. Sandy reaffirmed my interest and established a date and a time for the field rep to visit. She also got further details about my needs, which incidentally, had changed. Initially, I wanted an estimate on the walkway. My interest had included a landscaped patio. No small change. Score yet another for Sandy.

The appointment was for 2:00 p.m., and at 2:00 p.m. on the dot the doorbell rang. Was I impressed or what?! At last a well-coordinated inside and outside marketing program. I could have wept. Heh, where do I sign?

The joy was short-lived.

I went outside with the field rep, David (Who, as it turned out, was also the owner of the company). As we walked onto the grass, David said, "I don't like interlocking brick."

"Oh?," I gasped, alarmed, shocked, dumbfounded, astounded, and astonished.

"Yeah," he said, "Gotta bad back. Didn't want to do any brick this summer. But ya' know, with this economy . . ."

Although I listened politely and went through the motions, my decision had been made. The sale was lost.

But, the idea for this chapter began to form in my mind; I decided to make the best of the situation. "Richard, I received a call for your services from Sandy. Is she your lead generator?"

"My what?", he replied. "Oh yeah. She does all the calling for me."

"So how has she done so far?" I asked.

"Well, not very good. I hired her to save time by creating appointments for me. She makes appointments all right, but none of them have turned into sales. I don't think telephoning works too well in my line of business."

I needn't continue.

So, what's my point? All your professional telephone skills will not amount to a hill of beans unless everyone else does their job. What do you do about it? Simply put, work together. All campaigns should be planned jointly. Objectives should be established. Create scripts together. Develop a feedback system. Weekly or even daily reviews should be made. Consider a follow-up call to the customer after the visit. Obviously the key ingredient is communication. Work as a team and watch your sales grow.

57

Don't Lose Sales Because of Bad Timing

You might have the best script, the best techniques, the best product, and the winningest telephone personality, but if the timing of your offer is off, your efforts will not bear fruit.

Here is an example on a business-to-consumer level that happened to me personally in January. I received a call from the lawn care company that serviced my yard the previous year. It began pleasantly as a customer satisfaction survey. I was extremely pleased with the service and told them so. The sales rep asked if I would be using them in the future. Yes, probably. Then suddenly, BOOM, he tried to close me.

Understand this: I was well-targeted, being a previous user of their services. I was very impressed with their efforts. I said I would be using them again. Call me a mad cap crazy, but when I looked out the window at the five feet of snow swirling and twirling around the gray, barren trees with the temperature at about twenty below, the thought of lawn care was not predominant. Furthermore, when I glanced at the Christmas bills piled neatly by the phone, the thought of coughing up a few bucks for services to be rendered in about six months seemed incongruent.

So I told the telephone rep that I was involved in telesales and asked how the campaign was going. "Not so good," he replied. "I've made eighty-one calls and no one is ready even though we are offering to pay the GST (a Canadian government tax of 7%).

He seemed genuinely puzzled. I felt badly for him because he was obviously burning out. When I told him that the middle of winter in Canada was not the best time to sell lawn care, he actually seemed astounded. He said he would talk to his boss.

Well, it's June. I hear birds singing. I see the grass. I feel the warmth of the sun. I smell the earth. But I have yet to get a call. I have no doubt they have branded telesales as a failure. Too bad; the same call now would have been an entirely different result.

Lesson: Take a look at the products and services you sell. Is there a seasonal factor? Too often we get caught up with the everyday chore of selling and consequently forget to look at the big picture. Think about it.

And if your business is seasonal, you might want to use the time to "cultivate" the relationship. Make two or three calls in the preseason. By doing so, this rep could have gotten a feel for my lawn care needs. Perhaps identify a problem or two. Maybe educate me on products and solutions. And that would have built my trust once spring had arrived. It makes sense: the chances of closing a prospect who knows you and your company will increase dramatically.

58

"I Haven't Read it Yet."

How to Get Them Involved on Follow-Up Calls

Think of how many times the following has happened to you.

Caller: "Mr. Smith, I am just following up on that brochure and price list you requested."

Customer: "Oh, well . . . . I haven't gotten around to reading it."

It is a common occurrence that can discourage the best of sales reps. But it is nothing more than another objection that must be tackled. Establishing another follow-up call date is not the answer.

Being prepared, of course, is the answer. Try thinking of a follow-up call to direct mail or fulfillment piece as nothing more than a magnifying glass. The trick is to get the customer who has not read the piece to pick it up and have him or her focus on a particular item, section, fact . . . or whatever. Don't worry about selling or creating an appointment at this precise moment. Your objective is simply to get the customer to physically handle the piece. Let's continue from above.

Caller: "I know what you mean. My desk is piled high with mail. And that's why I am calling. To save you some time, I highlighted some items on the inside front cover of the brochure. If you take a quick look you will see the precise specs for the T-62 as you requested compared to the T-34 and Mark IV's."

First key point: The sales rep informally acknowledges that reviewing mail can be a tedious task. This is a human touch. And that's why the highlighting is key. Highlighting is a great way to focus attention and it saves the customer the hassle of poring through scads of copy.

Second key point: The sales rep ties that benefit into his remarks. The customer will save time. And the sales rep makes sure the customer understands this. It is a value-added component.

Third point: It forces the sales rep to focus on the customer's wants and needs. In essence, it acts as a road map for the call.

This simple tip can be invaluable when you run into the busy decision maker. The next time you send a fulfillment piece, take the time to mark the portions which are relevant to the customer's needs.

59

How to Stand Out From all the Sales Clutter

I had never been more popular in my life. When I started my own consulting firm, the phone didn't stop ringing. Salespeople called with everything from office supplies to computer accessories. Quite frankly, after two weeks, the calls all began to sound the same: boring. I was becoming immune to every pitch because they were identical; correct in every way, but clones of each other.

That is . . . until I got a call from Glen Weiers, who demonstrated a way to get past the clutter, make a presentation, and close the sale.

An Unexpected Package

It began with a couriered package delivered to my office. Inside the box I discovered a coffee cup emblazoned with his company's logo. Inside the cup was a packet of instant coffee, a small powdered creamer, two sugar packets and a small handwritten note. It read:

> "Mr. Domanski, congratulations on your new business venture! I am sure you have a lot on the go, but I thought you might like to take a break and join me for a coffee. I will join you with a call on Oct. 2nd at 10:15 a.m."

Well, who could resist? It was so unique that I actually grabbed my day planner and quickly wrote down the time. I said to myself, "Ah, now here is a great idea. Let's just wait and see if he has the follow-up punch."

The Call Arrived

Friday rolled around and shortly after ten, I received a call from Glen.

"Mr. Domanski, it is Glen Weiers calling from ABC Computing. Are you ready for that coffee?"

There was no benefit statement, and, in theory, I had no reason to listen. But it was such a charming approach that I wanted to hear what he had to say. So we had the coffee and got down to business. As a salesperson he was quite good—I purchased a laser printer and a few related items.

You Must Be Unique

The point here is simple. There are a lot of people calling your prospects and customers.

In such a competitive environment you must constantly think of ways to add value, uniqueness, and quality to your call. In today's competitive marketplace, the average salesperson is pretty well-equipped on the skills side. And while this quality telesales is great for us customers, it has also made it difficult to differentiate you and your products and services (unless you have a major competitive advantage such as price).

Glen (or his company) invested a few bucks in his strategy. I guess it paid off; the sale was $3500. And more importantly, Glen will likely get the next sale . . . and the sale after that. He invested in a relationship by using a little imagination.

What can you come up with?

60

How to Collect on What You Sell

M any of us are paid on commission—only after the customer pays the bill.

Yet, there are also many reps who bellyache about how customers take so long paying, therefore delaying their commission check. So why not call them personally?

Sure, some reps do, but others pooh-pooh the notion, muttering it is beneath them, and that it might damage their relationship with the customer.

Nonsense. What might be damaged is their relationship with their mortgage holder if too many customers are too late in payment.

Customer Service

Telephone collections when used in a planned and structured way can help you maintain and speed up cash flow (yours and the company's), and foster improved customer relations. A sensitive rep can acquaint new customers with company accounting procedures, ascertain the status of overdue accounts, and in the case of valued, old customers, determine why payment is being delayed.

If there is a problem, it's better that you fix it quickly, and calling them is a cost-effective way to do that.

A major hotel in Canada had been using a combination of mail and phone calls to collect its receivables. The hotel's 61-90 days past dues accounted for 10% of its receivables, with another 7% in the 91-120 overdue category. While this was on par with the rest of the industry, they decided to do something more formal to see if they could speed up the process.

With the new system, all outstanding bills of $250 and over were called at 30 days. If full payment could not be made, planned payments were scheduled. After 10 months, the bad debts over 90 days were virtually eliminated, and those in the 61-90 day category reduced to less than 1%. The savings in interest alone were considerable.

One of the keys for the hotel, and for you, is that the calls are positioned as service calls. They would call major accounts several days after the bill arrived just to make sure it was correct, and that everything was satisfactory. Apart from ensuring the bill was paid promptly, the calls also provided direct feedback on the hotel.

Sure, complaints were voiced, but those were complaints they might not have heard otherwise, and meant they had a chance to get that customer to come back. You can do the same thing.

Finally, think about some of the sales opportunities which may result from the calls. You probably wouldn't want to call just to sell, but undoubtedly, some of these customers will say, "While I have you on the phone . . ."

I heard a wise old sales manager one time say, "It isn't a sale until the check is in hand." You can ensure and quicken that process, while also building the customer relationship.

61

Nudging Your Customers and Prospects Along So They'll Do SOMETHING

Customers have good intentions when it comes to buying. But what customers sometimes lack is the drive and initiative to **act**. And these customers may rely on you to provide that drive. In essence, they need to be reminded and they need to be "pushed." I'm not taking about an aggressive shove, but rather an ever-so-gentle nudge. I am talking about **persistence.**

A case in point: Sheila, a telephone sales rep for a major new publication called me about running an ad late in the fall. I had run one (over $5K) at an earlier date, so I was an existing, qualified customer. I said I was interested but not until February. I would have both the budget and the opportunity because they were running a supplement on telemarketing. I told the rep to call me in January. I received a call in early January, but there was not the sense of urgency for me and I asked for a call later in the month.

Unfortunately, there was no call and I had forgotten about the whole thing even though it was important. Finally, something sparked me into calling Sheila. I asked why she had not called. "Oh, I did not think you were really interested." I just managed to slip in on time. Had I missed it ... egg on my face.

Sure, it was ultimately my responsibility but I expect a good sales rep to be my "partner" especially when we already have a relationship.

As I write this, I can recall countless examples where sales reps failed to nudge the prospect along. Shopping for business cards, I called a major business forms company. The lead was passed to a sales rep, who in turn, called and left a message. That was the end of it. No more calls. No fax. Not a single letter or contact. Later I learned that the sales rep felt that leaving a single message was sufficient. Not so.

Persistence is Partnering

Contrast this to Toby, a rep who was providing another service. You could set your watch by Toby's follow-up. On time, all the time. At times I was even slightly annoyed because she was the voice of my conscience as I tried to procrastinate certain decisions. Toby's manner was good natured. She acknowledged, tongue-in-cheek, that she was a pest but reminded me of the benefits and of the consequences if I missed certain dates. But it was this gentle prodding that made the whole project a big success. I looked good. And consequently, Toby will be a "partner" who will get more business. She helped me get things done.

Sometimes we get discouraged when our follow-up calls do not result in immediate action. It gets easy to ignore the next one. Yes, some customers are simply putting you off, but there are others who rely on you to help get things done.

The point: one "secret" to telesales success is, follow-up, follow-up, follow-up.

62

Do as I Say, Not as I Do

Remember one thing about this book:
Do what I say . . . not what I do.

It's always a little humbling when you don't follow your own advice. I'm afraid I blundered, but it helps illustrate a key point in telesales. Here's what happened.

In December a prospect called inquiring about training and/or consulting within his call center. We had established good rapport and I gladly sent the requested information to the prospect (Ken). I made a follow up call just before Christmas at which time Ken said he had not reviewed the information and suggested I give him a call in early January. This I did. Here's how it went:

> *"Ken, it's Jim Domanski from Teleconcepts Consulting in Ottawa. Ken you had asked me to call regarding the training and consulting proposal I had sent just before Christmas."*
>
> "Oh yeah," replied Ken rather vaguely. "Uhh, aahh . . . yeah, well, ah, we don't have anything planned for consulting or training at this time, but, ah, I'll keep the stuff on file."

I mumbled and fumbled a bit, and that was the way the call ended.

Kind of like a train wreck.

Analysis

Okay let's dissect what I did and did not do.

My opening statement was bland. While I identified myself and my company, the reason for my call was uninspiring.

177

And, it doesn't take a bash to the forehead from a Louisville Slugger to realize I did not provide a single benefit statement.

So, strike one.

My timing was also lousy. The first week of the New Year is often a poor time to call, if only because everyone more or less is getting themselves back into the swing of things. I am not saying you shouldn't call; rather I'm suggesting that this time of year requires a little more forethought.

Strike two.

Compounding my errors was my pre-call planning—I should say lack thereof. My opening statement proved that. It doesn't stop there; I did not have questions or rebuttals prepared when I encountered his objection. I was so flabbergasted that I was speechless. No contingency planning.

Strike three and I was out. Big time!

Complacency: The Plague of Veteran Reps

The problem on this call is easily spotted: I didn't think. I won't beat myself up over this because I recognize that problem is frequent, particularly with experienced reps. And that's my whole point. As experienced selling professionals our biggest problem tends to be that of complacency. We feel we know the stuff inside and out. We get comfortable in our habits. We even get lazy. And little by little we bend the rules until they break. That's what I did. I got lazy and I broke the rule about pre-call planning.

What Should I Have Done?

1. Obviously, I should have considered the issue of timing. Given that it was the first week in the new year I probably should have called later in the week. By then most people are back in the daily grind of business.

2. I should have carefully reviewed my notes and my proposal and developed a plan of action. I should have developed, either in my mind or on paper, a list of anticipated responses. (After all, a prospect can only have three attitudes: acceptance, rejection

or objection.) I should have anticipated the curve ball.

3. My opening statement needed more zip. For instance, I knew that Ken had just taken over the job as the call center manager and he explained how overwhelmed he was in assessing the staff, their results etc. I could have used this as leverage in my call. I could have recreated the "pain" that he expressed in December.

4. I should have rehearsed the call in my mind. Especially the opening. Could've role played the scenario. At this point, I wonder how my voice contributed to the call. Was it upbeat or did it have the New Year's blah?

The Teacher Becomes the Student: Can You Help Me?

If you were me, what would you have done? Should I have closed up my consultancy and moved to a monastery in Tibet?

Or should I have been mindful of the lesson I just learned and not do it again?

How about pursuing Ken and giving it another go?

If I were to pursue Ken, how do you think I should have approached the situation? Should I have written him a follow up letter? If so, what should I have said? Or perhaps, I should have skipped the mail and called him directly?

What would your opening statement say? I would love to know. What is your advice? Be the teacher/consultant. Take time to come up with your recommendation. In the next chapter you'll be able to compare your suggestions with those of your peers.

Moving Forward

In the meantime, let's emphasize a few points. First of all, pre-call planning is the very heart of any successful telephone sales call. It is like a pregame warm up before a sporting event. Without the warm-up you can perform, but chances are, your performance is not likely to be spectacular. Admittedly, pre-call planning can be a bit of a pain for the experienced reps who have managed to convince themselves that they don't need to do it. However, the pain of embarrassment is somewhat more intense than the pain of pre-call planning.

Don't ever forget the basics. And remember: Do what I say and not what I do!

63

Unbotching the Botched Call

When the previous chapter originally appeared as a column in the *Telephone Selling Report* newsletter I invited readers to respond with their suggestions. Boy, does misery love company? The response was, well, overwhelming!

Misery Loves Company

All the calls and faxes I received were from "veteran" sales reps, and, to a person, they all commiserated. They've all experienced the same type of call at various points in their careers. At least this supports my supposition that veteran sales reps can suffer from complacency from time to time.

Second, veteran sales reps are veterans because they continue to "sharpen" the saw. They continue to build and hone their skills regularly by reading books and newsletters such as *Telephone Selling Report.* They don't just sit on their duffs all day.

Everyone who responded felt I should pursue the prospect with a call. This got me thinking that the most successful sales reps have a couple of interesting traits. First, the ability to recognize they are not perfect; they make mistakes. They recognize them, accept them and learn from them. Then they move on. They don't dwell on botched calls. It's resiliency.

Successful and effective sales reps are persistent. A good rep recognizes and learns from the mistake. But a great sales person goes one step further and makes another call or two to that difficult prospect. They stare the botched call in the eyes and take another shot at it. Many times they turn it around.

Suggestions From the Vets

Sara from Toronto suggested I join the Tibetan monastery . . . if I didn't bother to follow up. Her serious suggestion was to send a letter with a copy of the preceding chapter in this book. Joanne, also from Toronto, felt this would be a great "positioning" strategy. In other words, if I could recover in this manner just imagine how I could help Ken's sales reps. This would be followed up by a *well-prepared* telephone call. I like that.

Eddie from Nashville focused on my lame handling of the prospect's excuse about not reviewing the literature before Christmas. He uses technology to overcome similar objections. Eddie has created a one page faxable summary sheet of various products and service offerings. When the prospect balks with such an objection Eddie taps a function key on his computer and . . . ZAP! The summary sheet transmits immediately. He says to the prospect,

> "Oh, that's no problem at all. Even as we speak I have a summary page faxing to you that details my literature and will save you some time. We can review it together."

Good idea Eddie. And fine benefit statements.

Prospects and Perspective

From the Chicago area, Steve and Dave gave another perspective. They pointed out that often we are too hard on ourselves. They explained that a prospect might be having a bad day and their remarks to the sales rep may in no way be a true reflection of anything we did or said by phone. Their real point was that giving up after one call was ridiculous.

Jim Felt from Minneapolis echoed his brethren in Illinois. He pointed out that prospects have existing "attitudes, moods and frames of mind at the time of call." He said it is the responsibility of the sales rep to overcome these attitudes with correct questioning and benefits.

Jim wasn't quite done with me. In his fax he gently chided me that I let Ken off much too easily with the ever elusive "I-have-not-reviewed-the-information" excuse. Here is a reply that Jim crafted.

182

64

What to Do When You Don't Get the Sale

Have you ever worked your tail off to get a sale? You know the ones. You did everything: cold called, direct mailed, followed up on time and with value, developed a quote or proposal, handled the objections, created another proposal with modifications . . . the whole nine yards . . .

. . . .and then, after days, weeks (or even months) the prospect drops the bomb on you. He tells you "Thank you. You did a great job. But we have chosen someone else. We're going with Company B."

What do you do?

How do you respond?

A lot hangs in the balance at this point. I have witnessed some reps who respond by shifting into a "sell mode" again. It's as if they believe that one more shot of features and benefits will convince the prospect to change his or her mind. It's pathetic, really.

Others are somewhat petulant. They are the ones that sarcastically reply "Fine," and more or less leave it at that. It's embarrassing.

Others still, take the cheap-shop artist approach with a remark like, "Company B is a good company—if you like lousy quality." That's downright shameful.

But the majority of reps murmur something vague, maybe a thanks, and then drift into oblivion and despair. And that's just plain sad.

Losing a big one is tough. But none of these responses are satisfactory. They are guaranteed to close the door on any future opportunity you might have. Here are some tips on how you or your company might improve on its next bid.

1. Listen

Most prospects recognize that you did a good deal of work and they usually feel compelled to explain why you didn't win the business. At this point you might get honest-to-goodness tips on how you or your company might improve on its next bid.

2. Express Disappointment, But With Dignity

> "Well, Mr. Masson, I must tell you I am disappointed . . ."

Not only does it show grace in defeat, it shows the measure of your effort and commitment to the sale.

3. Compliment The Customer On His Choice

To continue the above line,

> " . . . but I think you will not be disappointed with Company B. They have some good products and services."

Now I know this is tough, especially if you believe you have the very best product or service. But by reassuring the prospect that he or she made a wise choice, you make them feel good. And why, pray tell, would you do this? Well it is simple. You never know, the prospect might become disillusioned with company B. And who do you think he or she might call?

4. Send A Little Note

Say something like,

> "Mike, thank you for the opportunity to quote. I regret I did not have the chance to do some business at this point, but I suspect we'll be speaking to one another again . . ."

5. Give a Value-Added Component

> "Mike, listed below are three excellent books on

strategic positioning. You can get them at most bookstores. I thought you might find them handy with the project . . ."

Something like that is classy. Professional.

6. Leave The Door Open

"If I can be of any help, please give me a call. In the meantime, I would like to give you a call every now and then just to keep tabs on things . . ."

7. Then DO it

If you say you will call, set a time and do so. At least for a little while. Show him or her that you are a person of your word. Get them to say "WOW!"

Of course, you should not necessarily do this for every sale you lose. That would be ridiculous. I am talking about the sales that had high value, or sales where you placed your whole heart and soul into the effort.

Always remember, you have a choice when dealing with this type of situation. On the one hand you can behave like a child and lose all respect (and any future consideration). Or you can behave like an adult (and more specifically, like a professional) and possibly reap the long-term reward.

Which do you think is the right choice?

65

Eight Reasons Why Your Calls are Not Returned

The indignant telesales rep, Mark, said, "Well, I left him a message on his voice mail but I still haven't had the courtesy of a reply"

"Ya, I know what you mean. They use voice mail to screen your calls," consoled the equally dejected Sylvie.

Voice mail. Some sales reps say it's killing them. But I think the real trouble is that most reps give up a little too easily. They psych themselves out by convincing themselves that the prospect cannot be even vaguely interested, otherwise they would have called back. Right?

Wrong.

There could be a number of reasons why the prospect hasn't returned your call. Here are a few to ponder.

1. The Message Was Not Received

I recently discovered that a half a dozen of messages left in my voice mail box were somehow eliminated, dumped or otherwise lost.

2. The Prospect Forgets

In a single morning I once had 17 messages. I prioritized them and called them in order. In the meantime, I handled other calls and business. The messages at the bottom of the priority pile slipped through the cracks.

3. Your Message is Unclear

Someone left me a message a few days ago that was interesting . . . I think. The message was garbled due to bad transmission.

4. You Inverted Your Number

Believe it. It happens.

5. The Prospect Inverts Your Number

He or she is just as fallible as you.

6. Your 800 Number Might Not Be Accessible

I am subject to this on a weekly basis. I receive calls from people in the U.S. who assume their 800 line works from Canada. It often doesn't.

7. The Prospect is a Procrastinator

It is common enough. Let he who hath no sin, cast the first stone.

8. Come Up With Your Own Reasons

With a little thought, I am sure you could uncover more reasons why you should make that second, third or even fourth call. Jot them down along with the seven I have given you. The next time you are faced with a dose of call reluctance after you have left a voice message, review these points. Use them to psych yourself up. Not every customer hides behind a voice mail screen so pick up the phone and dial again!

We have covered reasons why your calls are not returned. Now we're ready, in the next chapter, to talk about ideas you can use on voice mail to combat these problems, and get more buyers to call you back.

66

How to Win The War On Voice Mail

I f there is one single question asked over and over again in my training seminars its is: "How do you deal with voice mail?"

There is perhaps no greater "enemy" to cold calling today than voice mail. To me, voice mail is like a huge fortress with thick walls preventing sales reps from reaching the prospect. Getting past voice mail is not unlike preparing a major military campaign. It involves strategy and tactics, guile and determination, persistence and patience.

Three Strategies

There are three strategies that can be employed when you encounter voice mail. They should be followed sequentially i.e., if Strategy One fails, move to Strategy Two. If that comes up empty, move to Strategy Three.

Strategy One: Avoid It

The objective of this strategy is to avoid voice mail completely and attempt to reach your prospect live. That is right, when you encounter voice mail, don't leave a message. At least not initially.

The first thing you should do is gather "intelligence." Listen to the prospect's message and note its contents carefully. Does the prospect state his or her name and ask that the caller leave a message? Or does the prospect state their name and the current date and then asks the caller to leave a message?

In the latter case, you have managed to get a key piece of information: the prospect changes his message daily. What this means to you is that the prospect reviews his messages daily. It

the piece. Remember, faxes have a sense of urgency to them.

Summary

Although e-mail is catching up, the fax is still the darling of the business world—but it is getting a little worn. To make it an effective selling tool, review your current use of the fax. Is it different from all the rest? Can you improve the use of the medium? Doing so could make all the difference in meeting your sales objectives.

69

Wayne Gretzky and Role Playing

Anyone who knows me will tell you I have a fascination—no, an obsession—with the Great One, the hockey player Wayne Gretzky. I love to watch him. I try to emulate him.

When Gretzky played with the Los Angles Kings, the team held their training camp in my city. I was the first in line to watch the practices hoping to pick up some tips that would make me the "Great One" on Sunday nights in my own local hockey league.

I scrutinized everything he did. I watched him skate up and down. I noted the way he stretched. I studied how he performed the skating and shooting drills over and over and over again. It suddenly occurred to me that my buddy Wayne was doing what everyone else was doing: drills. He was practicing simple passing patterns and he took the same shot over and over. He skated the same patterns time and again.

What About Telesales?

Okay so what does my hero worship have to do with telesales? The key to my Sunday hockey night success did not lie with picking up a few tips; it is in practicing.

In the same vein, the key to telesales success does not depend on simply reading a book like this one and getting a few tips. The key to success lays in practicing and applying what you have learned. You do that through role playing.

Role playing is the training camp of telesales. It's grunt work. It is the time to try new techniques; it is time to rehearse old techniques. It is practice, practice over and over again, ad nauseam.

At the camp, the Kings had invited a number of rookies from their minor league teams to practice with them. Watching these rookies practice with the team was not unlike watching a couple of sales reps who were practicing their scripts in the training room next to my office. Both the reps and the hockey rookies attacked and devoured their drills. They were keen on making "the team" so they worked hard.

And watching some of the veteran Kings players practicing also reminded me of several veteran reps I happen to know. Both sets of veterans had experienced the big times and though they practiced their skills, the intensity was not nearly the same.

Intensity and Determination

But as I watched Wayne, who, as I write this, is a seasoned but yet still prolific veteran, and has broken every possible hockey record, I saw the same intensity and determination of a rookie. Undoubtedly, Wayne has been blessed with talents that most hockey players only dream about. But I suspect that what truly makes Wayne a "great one" is his commitment to practicing and playing hard.

In his autobiography Gretzky states that parents have come up to him with their kids and say, "Wayne, tell my son to practice three hours a day like you did." Wayne explains that no one told him to practice three hours a day. He practiced all day because he loved it. Wayne still maintains that the greatest compliment you can pay him is to say he worked hard, practice or game, and that he never dogged it.

I am not suggesting that you have to have the same devotion for telesales as Gretzky has for hockey. However, I am suggesting that Wayne is as good as he is, and for as long as he has been because he continues to practice basic fundamental hockey skills. Role playing in telesales is not something that should be cast aside once you have hit the big times. Role playing, even if it is only for a few minutes per day, is the way to maintain and sharpen your fundamental telesales skills. Practicing through role playing is your opportunity to try new approaches. Be it a simple opening statement, or a whole new script, the place to practice is with your manager or your peers. Not with your customers. The time to make the mistakes is in your training session, not with one of your most valued clients.

Watching the G-Man made me realize something else: It made me realize that I wanted a quick fix" for my own brand of hockey. I thought by watching him closely, I would learn to finesse the puck and work magic behind the net. Sales reps do the same thing: they hear of something that worked for others and they give it a try. For the most part, if the technique does not work it is written off. There is no quick fix to my hockey career and there is no quick fix to becoming a good sales rep. There is only work and practice.

The next time you are faced with the drudgery of role playing, just remember Wayne Gretzky. Remember how he got there and how he has stayed there.

Section Ten: How to Get and Stay Motivated

70

How To Overcome Fear on the Phone, and of the Phone

It was Mark Twain, I believe, who said that courage was not the absence of fear, but rather the *mastery* of fear.

Fear is a part of the telephone selling game. The curious thing about fear is that it can be a debilitating disease which can destroy confidence on the one hand, yet fear can also be a tremendously powerful motivator for sales success on the other. You have the power to choose how fear is used.

Types of Fears

If you have been in selling for any length of time you know what I am talking about. But just in case, let's reacquaint ourselves with just four of the more common fears.

> • **Fear of rejection.** Given the number of calls a sales rep can make by phone, rejection is usually the number one concern. People might not like us.

> • **Fear of closing.** It stems from rejection. If you close you might get rejected, so you don't close.

> • **Fear of objections.** Sales reps sometime interpret objections as some sort of indication of disapproval. The consequence? We hear an objection and we either give leave, or turn it into an adversarial situation.

> • **Fear of failure.** Lurking somewhere in our subconscious (or conscious) minds, is the ultimate fear of failure. If the sales rep doesn't make his objec-

tives, that somehow suggests a lack of self-worth.

So what do you do?

Tackling Fear Up Front

I wish there was some sort of powerful potion that you could ingest or some secret incantation that you could recite that would banish fear completely. Unfortunately there is not.

Here are some tips and techniques for dealing with your fears . . . whatever they might be.

1. Admit to it. There is nothing wrong with admitting that you have a fear. If the word "fear" bothers you, then call it a "concern" instead. Whatever. Just acknowledge that there is something that makes you uncomfortable. Identify it.

Turning a blind eye is not a solution. Once you know exactly where your fear lies, you are on the way to developing a positive action plan.

2. Increase your selling skill level. In most cases I have observed, fear is usually the result of a lack of skill in a given area. Objections handling and closing are very common as suggested above. Lack of skill means a lack of confidence. Fear breeds as quickly as mosquitoes in a swamp with those who lack confidence. Constantly work at developing your skills. Start by reading books on selling. Subscribe to the **Telephone Selling Report** newsletter if you don't already (800-326-7721, or, 402-895-9399). Listen to cassette tapes in your car. Go to your manager or supervisor. Tell them your concerns. Ask them to monitor your calls and get coaching. Taping your calls is also necessary. Create a "user group," a group of people with whom you can exchange ideas and practice. Find a mentor. Practice. Practice the techniques on your spouse, your cat or dog, your kids.

3. Build your "other" skills. Some reps are terrible letter writers. Some can't effectively cope with a computer and keyboard. These are things that can be overcome with formal and informal training. Is it grunt work? You bet. Get to it. If you are not sure, have the guts to ask someone who can give you a fair, objective opinion.

4. Increase your knowledge level. I will let you in on a trade secret: most sales reps are lazy when it comes to building their product knowledge. Most reps reach a comfort zone in product knowledge and go no further. You should become the "resident expert" on all your products. People love experts. Expertise brings confidence. Pick up the product and service manuals daily and read them. Memorize it if you have to. Examine every piece of literature (brochures, spec sheets, price lists). Review every piece of promotional material that goes into the customer's hand. Resident expert, remember?

5. Use the tools you have. There are sales departments where considerable time and effort have been invested in developing all sorts of job aids: scripts. call guides, objections manual, Feature-Advantage-Benefit sheets . . . which are distributed and then neatly stored away never to be used. Use the tools you have. They do work! And if you are uncertain about how useful they are, then stop complaining and do something about it. Make changes, edit, modify, revamp. Just do it and then use it.

6. Set objectives. Wow, what a novel idea! Sometimes we have every intention of setting objectives but never quite do. Sometimes we have vague objectives. And sometimes we have objectives that are simply too easy, or too impossible.

Realistic objective-setting drives us forward. More importantly, they act as a diagnostic tool. They are key indicators and tell us how we are doing and where we need to concentrate.

7. Plan. Plan. Plan. Plan. I am talking about planning in the very broadest sense. Start by planning your day the night before (Similar to objective setting). Know who you will be calling. Know why. Know when. Have your game plan laid out. Plan each and every call. All too often we get stuck in the rut of routine: treating every call the same. It ain't so! Review each file or screen before making the call. Make sure you know exactly who you will be calling. Sure it's grunt work—but also stuff you sometimes forget to do. Digging in and taking action makes you competent and efficient. It combats fear.

Combating fear is not particularly difficult. There are dozens of things that must be done daily on an ongoing basis. Most sales reps intuitively know this. So hunker down and master fear.

71

Use Visualization Techniques to Improve

I f you really want to take advantage of the ideas offered in this book, try visualization. Visualization is nothing more than a fancy word which, translated, means mentally rehearsing or practicing a newfound technique or method.

Sounds simple and easy doesn't it? And that is probably the reason why it is often ignored as a training technique. I suppose it is like the old tale about cough medicine: If it doesn't taste bad it must not be working. Unfortunately, its full potential has yet to be realized by trainers and salespeople alike.

Practice Regularly

However, visualization does work and it works well when practiced regularly. It is not a new, trendy pschyo-babble technique despite the name. Countless studies have revealed that your nervous system cannot tell the difference between an imagined experience and a real experience. If we imagine ourself performing in a certain manner, it is nearly the same as the actual performance.

Perhaps one of the most graphic and inspiring examples that demonstrates the power of mental practicing is the case of Major Nesmeth. The Major was a fighter pilot who was shot down over North Vietnam and spent seven years in a prison; most of it in solitary confinement. In an effort to preserve his sanity, Nesmeth played a full round of golf in his mind every morning. He envisioned every single detail such as addressing the ball, adjusting his stance, controlling his swing, keeping his head down, hearing the sound of the club against the ball and watching the ball fly straight and true down the fairway. It took the Major four hours to go through the entire game.

Prior to Vietnam, Nesmeth had always been a duffer; he shot somewhere in the 90's. Shortly after he was released, Major Nesmeth went onto the course, and, after seven years of not even physically touching a club, shot an incredible 74!

Repetitive Experiences

Teleselling and servicing is nothing more than a series of situations. The more experience you have with a certain situation, the better equipped you are to handle it. By mentally rehearsing various situations, you are, in effect, getting actual experience. Practice the techniques and ideas that you've learned in the safety and comfort of your own mind. Set aside twenty or thirty minutes on the way to and from work (if you're not driving!); at lunch; before bedtime; in the shower; anywhere. Close your eyes. Relax. See yourself on the phone. Picture a situation with a customer such as dealing with an objection or handling an irate customer. Envision yourself successfully utilizing a technique you have learned. Hear the happy customer. Feel the satisfaction of doing a good job. The nice thing about a mental rehearsal is that there is no risk. You cannot embarrass yourself and you always win. This helps create a positive mental attitude which helps to gain the confidence to actually try the new method or techniques in a real-life situation.

72

The Stanislawski Method of Motivation

O K, we're all in agreement you need to be motivated to excel at anything—especially telesales. But understand one thing: no one can motivate you. **You** are the only one who can motivate yourself. Salary, commission, bonuses and incentive programs create a motivating environment, but the desire (the motivating factor) comes from within. Here are some tips on self-motivation.

An acquaintance of mine, Rob, is the president of a fundraising company that focuses on raising money for symphonies, museums and the like. He shared with me a training technique that they vigorously teach their telesales reps. It is called the Stanislawski Method of Motivation. I like it. It works for me. It might for you, too.

Similar to Visualization

The Stanislawski Method is not unlike the visualization techniques we already discussed. But whereas visualization seeks to get the individual to "see" himself or herself performing the job or basking in a successful manner, Stanislawski teaches that the individual should recall successful events in one's life or job just prior to performing a task. His theory is that the mind should be "fertilized" and "nurtured" with positive thoughts.

In terms of a telesales environment, Stanislawski would suggest that before you pick up the phone and dial, take two or three minutes to simply relax and think of your past successes. In essence, you are molding a positive attitude with real events

213

in your life. The operative words are "your past successes."

Rob suggests that you take a sheet of paper, or a small card and that you list all your major accomplishments to date. Don't be shy. Brag about yourself. It is a personal document meant for your eyes only. Keep this card handy in your wallet or in your purse. Update it as more accomplishments come to be. You use it when you are about to make your first call or if you feel a slump coming on.

Just for kicks, I listed my personal accomplishments and one day, just before a major presentation, I hauled the list out of my pocket and concentrated on it for a few minutes. When I went back on stage I was really "pumped" up. The seminar presentation was a hit. Whether this was wholly due to Stanislawski, I am not sure. But I firmly believe it was another piece in that complex puzzle that gave me an "edge."

73

"Use the Force, Luke."

Lessons From a Jedi Master on Motivation in Telephone Sales

The other day I found my son Kevin in front of the TV, elbow deep in a vat of buttered popcorn, watching the great movie classic, Star Wars.

I joined him just as Luke Skywalker attacked the dreaded Death Star. The young Jedi was caught in a maze of corridors with Imperial fighters swarming all about him, attempting to launch a missile down a narrow chute. Luke was frustrated and discouraged and all looked lost when suddenly the spirit of the great Jedi master, Obi-Wan Kanobi uttered the words "Use the Force, Luke." Well, we know the rest of the story. Luke used the "Force" and promptly destroyed the Death Star.

While you don't quite face Imperial fighters, your job is probably no less challenging than that of the rebels fighting the Empire. We get discouraged. We even think of giving up. Luke used the "Force" to overcome his challenges. You can too. This chapter is about using the "Force" in telesales. How to create and tap into that inner drive; how to keep the motivation alive.

Luke learned many lessons from Obi-Wan Kanobi, but perhaps the greatest lesson was that the "Force" lay within Luke himself. What this means to you is that no one—not your supervisor, not your manager, not your peers—can motivate you. Only you can motivate yourself.

If Obi-Wan were here today, here are the lessons he might impart:

Lesson I: Determine Your Mission

Creating the "Force" starts with a clear focus. All Jedi Knights had focus. You must have a vision or a mission that acts as an overall target; a sense of direction.

Start by creating your own mission statement relative to the job. Believe me, it drives you. For example, one rep I trained, Frank, had written a simple yet powerfully effective mission statement that read,

> *"My mission is to be the best outbound sales rep in the company."*

Write your own statement on paper. Try it now. It doesn't hurt.

My Mission in telesales is: _____

Post it somewhere. Review it daily.

Lesson 2: Set Your Goals

Obi-Wan would likely tell you that goals bring even greater focus and concentration. While Luke's mission was to eliminate tyranny in the Empire, some of his initial goals were to save Princess Leia and to destroy the Death Star. Goals are simply steps to achieving the mission.

You can, and should, have any number of goals. One is revenue related. But goals can also relate to other aspects such as commission, training and education . . . whatever it takes to achieve your mission.

You bring the same sort of narrowed focus to your job. For example, Frank's revenue goal was to generate a $250,000 revenue for that year. Note that his goal was both specific and measurable. Your goals must be the same, but they must also be challenging, yet attainable. Try it right now.

My goals to achieve my mission are:

_____

Lesson 3: Break the Goal into Manageable Parts

Goals are typically big. Saving a princess held captive by nasty Imperial Stormtroopers is pretty tough. And forget about blowing up a Death Star the size of a small planet. Sales reps can easily lose the "Force" if they get too daunted by the size of the overall goal.

A quarter of a million dollars sounds like a lot. But what Frank did was break his goal into manageable parts, or objectives. For instance, the monthly goal was less than $21,000. The weekly: $5200. Per day, just over a thousand dollars in revenues. Here again, we see the narrowing of the focus and the "concentration of power." Your "Force" is then concentrated into a much smaller, realistic and attainable objective.

Chop your goals into manageable parts. Don't worry about being exact. Just do it and familiarize yourself with the process.

Lesson 4: Create a Plan

Luke Skywalker would not have lasted a nanosecond if he simply hopped into the X-Wing fighter and attacked the Death Star. No, Luke and the Rebels had a specific plan of attack and in telesales, you need the same thing. All too often I have seen reps hop into their chairs and pound the phones. It is aimless . . . without direction. Eventually it creates discouragement because goals are not met. And with discouragement comes burnout.

A plan creates discipline because it tells us precisely how you will achieve the objectives. It's what keeps the "Force" flowing. Here are a few examples of what I mean:

- ❏ Review prospect list daily
- ❏ Send initial letter to 10 new prospects/day
- ❏ Make 30 complete calls per day
- ❏ 10 cold calls per day (i.e., follow up to direct mail)
- ❏ 20 calls to existing clients
- ❏ Complete paperwork for all sales
- ❏ Plan/schedule next day

Consistent planning leverages your time and increases your focus (there's that word again). A plan means results.

Lesson 5: Increase Your Knowledge

Luke had raw skills when it came to handling his light sabre. But in order for him to effectively wield it he flew off to some desolate planet to learn more with the help of Yoda, that dwarf-like creature. In your case, develop your "Force" by building your knowledge by reading extensively and broadly about selling. Purchase tapes on motivation, goal setting and sales... and then listen to them. Often! These are steps on becoming a "master." The more you know, the greater your confidence level, and the better your results.

Lesson 6: Develop and Practice Skills

You might remember Luke practicing his swordsmanship while blindfolded. It is one thing to build your knowledge base but it is quite another to build your skill level. Skills are the practical application of knowledge. After you read of a technique, try it. Become familiar with the new skill by practicing it with friends or colleagues, or on your own.

In the movie, Luke actually got a little electrical jolt every time he missed one of the objects. As you try a new skill be prepared for uncomfortable jolts as you learn. Don't be discouraged. That's what practicing is for. Expect to feel some discomfort. Embrace it. When you feel discomfort you will know you are breaking out of your comfort zone and expanding your skill level.

Lesson 7: Seek Help

A moment ago, I mentioned Yoda. Yoda acted as a mentor and a guide for Luke to develop the Force. Find a coach who can give you advice and feedback. Sometimes it is a veteran rep. Sometimes it is a manager or supervisor. Sometimes it is someone outside of the office who can give you objectivity and perspective.

Lesson 8: Visualize

Here's that word again. Remember how Luke was blindfolded when practicing? He was learning to use his mind to see, feel and develop the techniques. You can do the same. Visualize yourself using a skill. Create scenarios in your mind and play them out. See yourself successfully handling an objection, presenting an idea, closing a sale . . . whatever.

Lesson 9: "Just Do It."

Develop an action orientation.

This means taking risks. While Luke spent some time on the planet practicing his skills, the time came when he simply had to go out and use what he learned. I mention this because I have seen my share of sales reps who are great readers, learners and "practicers" but never seem to implement the newfound techniques into their selling efforts.

Develop a "just do it" philosophy which means the only way you will really develop your skills is to try them in the real world. As you succeed, that internal drive (Force) builds momentum. You will learn to say "Hey, I did it." And with every "Hey, I did it" comes greater confidence to do more.

Lesson 10: Broadcast Your Intentions

I am not sure if Skywalker announced to all those around him that he was going to save Princess Leia or destroy Darth Vader & Company. But certainly Luke's demeanor suggested he had every intention of doing so. By telling those around you about your goals, you are placing a certain amount of stress upon yourself to succeed. Good stress. Good stress is another form of motivation. If you officially go "on record," others begin to watch.

And as they watch, you begin to push yourself to perform. Incidentally, try broadcasting your intentions to yourself. One technique I have seen is posting signs or notes around your work station. One rep in particular, Chris, taped his revenue objectives to his computer monitor. This "in your face" message is highly effective because it acts as a constant reminder of your goals and objectives.

Lesson 11: Reward Yourself

In Chris' workstation there was a picture torn from a travel brochure. It featured a palm tree looming over a long sandy beach bordered by a calm, aquamarine ocean. His reward for achieving his goals was a trip to Hawaii. Chris also developed his own series of interim rewards for achieving monthly goals. You might want to do the same.

In summary, Luke saved a princess, destroyed a Death Star and saved the Rebel Alliance by using "The Force." You can develop your own "Force" by learning the lessons taught here. The lessons are simply not enough. You need to put them into action. So, go to work.

74

The 8/1000th Solution: Developing an Edge

Now that I've been bitten by the golfing bug, it seems that everyone has advice on how I can improve my game. A well-intentioned fellow hacker gave me an old *Golf Digest* magazine with an article detailing how I could forever rid myself of this nasty hook. The article helped somewhat, but what really struck me were some of the statistics about players on the PGA tour.

The leading scorer from this particular season, several years ago, Payne Stewart (I told you it was an old copy of the magazine!) averaged 69.45 strokes per round. Greg Norman was second at 69.458. The difference between the players was a mere .008 or 8/1000th. The measurable difference between the two scores was small, but the outcome in terms of a game of golf, over the year, is significant.

In telesales being 8/1000th better than your competitor is measurably small, but the results over the course of a week, a month, and a year are significant.

The concept behind the ideas offered in this book are designed to give you a edge. Great or small, an edge is a competitive advantage in the world of telesales.

It reminds me of Jan Carlson's comments some years ago. Carlson, the dynamic CEO of Scandinavian Airlines who turned the company around from a disaster to a dynamo, commented that their success was not due to any one factor. He explained that they did not become 1000% better at any one thing but rather, they became 1% better at a thousand different things.

Just 1%!

How to Achieve an Edge

Here are little things that you can do gain an edge. Alone, they might not be significant. But as a whole, they become powerful tools for success

1. Read

Read everything you can about sales and teleselling. Scan magazines, newsletters, books and periodicals.

2. Write it Down

Once you read—or hear—something of value, big or small, record it right after you read or hear it. Don't trust it to memory.

3. Create an Edge Diary

Use a notebook, a loose leaf binder, your notebook computer, or create a special section in your daily calendar. Keep all of your tips in one handy place; divide the notebook into categories such as "Planning," "Opening Statements" "Questioning," etc.

4. Review

Set aside ten or fifteen minutes everyday (yes, everyday) to review the notebook. Get in the habit of monitoring yourself.

5. Initiative

Take the initiative when you have a problem, question or concern to call an expert. You will he surprised at the help you will get if you just ask.

6. Practice

Get in the habit of trying out the new idea with friends, peers and customers. Tape record yourself.

7. Be Patient

It takes about 21 days for a new habit to become ingrained. You have to consciously apply it during that time before it is natural.

8. Use Visualization

Rehearse your new technique in your mind while in the

shower, on the bus, at lunch.

Make this mental exercise part of your daily routine.

9. Establish Specific Goals

And develop a strategy to achieve them. For example, use; "post it" notes to remind yourself to cross-sell and upsell.

10. Reward Yourself

When you do something big or something small that adds to your repertoire of skills, reward yourself. Treat yourself royally.

11. Invest in Yourself

Take a self-development course. Buy yourself the necessary tools such as tapes, books, etc. (and don't always expect the company to pick up the tab). It is your life, so take responsibility for it.

Let me return to golf for a moment. I did take one small tip that has had a significant impact on my game. I opened my stance about one inch. One measly little inch! The result? That one inch adjustment has added about twenty yards to my five iron shot, about forty five to my driver, and my wedge shots actually loop into the air. Still working on that nasty bending hook . . .

Golf, like telesales, is a profession with many variables. Whoever is leading the PGA in scoring this week knows that his game is not based on any one single element but on all the elements combined. He knows that being just a bit better on all of the components of the game is all that he needs to win. And if you don't believe me, just ask Greg Norman.

Look for your own 8/1000th solution.

Section Eleven: Habits of Highly Effective Telephone Professionals

To conclude this book I'mpresenting my interpretation of Dr. Stephen Covey's immensely successful book, The *"7 Habits of Highly Effective People."* The book is not the latest in pop psychology or self-help, but rather it is a collection of sound principles which can assist an individual in leading an "effective" life.

The principles apply to our personal lives but over the next several chapters I will review the principles from the perspective of a telephone sales rep.

My objective is simply to get you to think in a different manner; to provide a new perspective. Much of the information is common sense; but common sense does not necessarily mean it is commonly applied. So let's get started.

75

Components Of a Habit

A habit is a principle that you internalize, and a principle is an idea that seems to make sense to most human beings.

A habit is comprised of three things: Skill, Knowledge and Desire, and it forms when these three components overlap.

A skill is knowing **how** to do something. Handling objections or closing the sale are skills. Knowledge is **knowing** what to do and why you should do it. For example, knowledge would apply to products and services. Desire, the final component, is also another name for attitude. It represents **wanting** to do something.

Habit

Desire

Skill

Knowledge

Let's put this all together for a moment. We know for example, that a sound business principle is "Value the Customer." It is an idea that makes sense to most people. You may have the proper skills-set to service the customer (probing skills, for example) and you may have knowledge of what to do in certain situations, and why. But if you don't want to value the customer—if you feel you are subservient or that you have never been treated the same way—then the skill and knowledge mean little.

In telephone selling you need all three components. But to be truly successful and excel in telephone selling, you need to *overlap* all three components so they become a habit.

Self-Analysis

First, you need to do a self analysis.

1. Do you have the skills to sell and service properly? If not, what will you do to get them? (See Habit 1, next chapter.)

2. Do you have the necessary knowledge to effectively sell and service your customer? If not, what do you plan to do about it?

3. Finally, do you have the desire to do the job? Do you like it? Do you want to do the job well? If not, you are in the wrong profession.

Take the time now to assess these three elements. Do you have a habit? Do you have the makings of a habit? What must you do to align and overlap these three components? Read on.

76

Habit One: Be Proactive

In the business world, being proactive means taking the initiative. But it also means taking responsibility. Take a closer look at the last word: "response-ability." In essence, it means "having the ability to choose a response." In *"The 7 Habits of Highly Effective People,"* Dr. Stephen Covey maintains that understanding you have a choice in how you respond to events around you is a simple but powerful concept.

A Matter of Choice

Let's look at an example. While monitoring calls, one of the reps, Derek, complained to me that his mediocre results were due to the fact that his manager was not providing enough coaching and training. Derek had even suggested that perhaps the company should subscribe to the **Telephone Selling Report** newsletter. However, his manager explained that such an expenditure was not in the budget. So Derek chose to blame his manager, the budget and his company for his results. Consequently, he was bitter and cynical.

I suggested to Derek that maybe *he* should invest in Art Sobczak's sales tips newsletter, **Telephone Selling Report** (call 800-326-7721 or 402-895-9399 for a free sample copy). In other words, that he be proactive and take responsibility for his own career development.

I also suggested that he had another choice: find a company that was more training- and development-focused.

Similarly, let's look at sales rejection. We have all experienced it. When we get into a rut where nothing seems to be going our way, we actually have a choice in how we react to the circumstance.

For example, we can:

- get depressed
- get ticked off at the customer
- blame your manager
- kick the dog
- become cynical
- become completely indifferent
- do nothing.

Or, you can be proactive and see the event as a learning experience.

Not PMA

Being proactive is a mental set. It is not simply forcing yourself to have positive mental attitude. While it is likely that you will feel better if you have a happy face than a sad one, no one is saying you can't get angry or annoyed, or down for awhile—it happens, and pretending it doesn't is delusional.

Being proactive is what you do after.

It is what you do to take charge. It is an acceptance or a realization that only *you* can control your response or reaction to events around you.

The Dereks of the world are victims. They are reactive people.

What Can You Do?

I wish there was some magic dust that would instantaneously make you proactive. There isn't. It comes from within. And once you have decided that you are the master of your own fate, there is a "liberating effect." You are on the road to becoming effective. It is important to understand that until you take responsibility, you cannot progress toward the next six habits.

So give your head a shake and be proactive.

77

Habit Two: Begin With the End In Mind

I asked the sales rep, "So, Randy, what do you want to be doing a year from now here at EMCOS? Do you want to get into supervision, field sales, marketing?"

"Ah, I dunno . . . never thought about it," the sales rep said, obviously befuddled by my question.

Poor Randy. He illustrates the value and importance of the second habit of highly effective sales reps: "Begin with the End in Mind." This means knowing exactly what you want to accomplish, where you want to go, what you want to become. It is goal setting on a larger scale. Covey calls it the "leadership" habit because it deals with longer-term direction.

So many of the reps I have met see themselves in a temporary—if not dead-end—job. With that kind of vision it is not difficult to see why sales results are mediocre, if not downright poor. The most successful reps I have met have a clear understanding of what they want to do and how they are going to achieve it.

Covey recommends a single but effective exercise which I suggest you try. Sit back and envision that you are at your own funeral three years from now; you're a spirit hovering over the congregation. A eulogy is being given by a fellow worker, by a customer, and by a boss. What is it you hope they would say? A hard worker? Ambitious? Skilled? Or would you rather hear; mediocre, lacked drive, no direction, drifter, sporadic? Is there a choice? IF you seriously participated in this exercise you will have touched on some of the values that are important to you in your career.

Don't tie yourself to your past, but rather to your potential . . . your future.

Concentrate not on what you are or were, but rather, on what you can be. Once you envision yourself as a field rep, a trainer, a supervisor or manager, you have developed direction. A vision. At this point it is simply a matter of plotting out the strategies to achieve the goal.

If you have read and adhered to "Habit One, Be Proactive," you will have understood that you are responsible for your destiny as a sales rep. Habit Two is simply an extension of Habit One. I think you will find this a very motivating and rewarding habit because it gives you something longer-term for which to shoot. It also reveals what you must do to achieve the goal; it shows the gap that must be bridged.

Here's an illustration that reveals what must be done to achieve your goal.

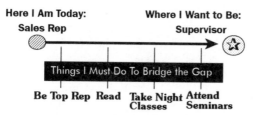

In this example the sales rep has his sights set on supervision but in order to achieve the goal, there are certain things that need to be done.

I've listed four but certainly there is more to it than that. Breaking the goal into sub goals makes the attainment of vision both manageable and achievable. It is not nearly as awesome as it may at first appear. You can build time frames and plot your success as you go. It is the *responsible* and *proactive* thing to do.

Take a moment now and plot your own graph before moving on to the next chapter.

78

Habit Three: Putting First Things First

Remember Randy, the sales rep I mentioned in the previous chapter? He was the one who wasn't quite sure what he wanted to do with his career. I was in his office again, and there he was faxing out some brochures at about 10:30 a.m.—prime calling time. I watched him for 15 minutes as he fed the sheets into the machine, one at a time. Still frustrated. Still in a fog. Still aimless in his pursuit of life. Randy has not yet learned the third habit.

Urgent and Important

The third habit of highly effective sales reps is "Putting First Things First." It is derived from the time management field, but Dr. Stephen Convey calls it the habit of personal management. What he really means is the ability to manage your everyday tasks and activities to achieve your goals (which we learned about in Habit Two). Any task or activity which is attached to the achievement of those goals are labeled "important."

However, most sales reps get caught up in "urgent" tasks and activities. These are things which seem to have a sense of "immediacy" to them. Things like faxing the brochure, mailing out the follow-up letters, discussing the latest objection, reviewing the newest product literature, or returning a phone call. Trouble is, not all urgent tasks are "important."

Highly effective sales reps recognize that there are four categories of tasks and activities as illustrated with the diagram on the facing page. Effective sales reps understand the implication of each quadrant and manage them accordingly. The first quadrant represents activities that are both urgent and important. They must be done or there will be serious consequences. Effective sales reps tackle these issues immediately. For example, an urgent and important task is completing your sales quota for the day.

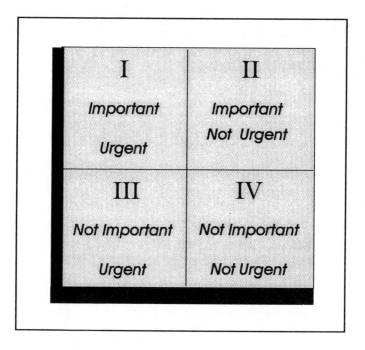

Meanwhile, the third quadrant reveals tasks that are urgent but not important. For example, unopened mail typically has a sense of urgency to it but rarely is the letter important to your goals.

The fourth quadrant consists of activities that are neither urgent nor important. These are the big time wasters like early morning gossip, reading the newspaper, and lingering over coffee.

The Key to Effectiveness

Quadrant II, then, is the key to effectiveness. Quadrant II represents important activities. But, unfortunately, there is no sense of urgency attached to them. And therein lies the problem. Without a sense of urgency, these activities tend to be put off. This is the downfall of most reps who have the desire to get ahead. They are unable to focus on those activities that will ultimately bring the most reward.

In the preceding chapter, we had listed the goal of becoming a supervisor. To achieve that goal we decided that you have to become the top rep, take night courses, read and attend seminars. That takes time and you are already swamped . . . busy putting out fires in Quadrant I, while tackling all those nagging time wasters of Quadrants III and IV.

The trick is that you must manage yourself and eliminate activities in Quads IV and III respectively to free up time for the achievement of your goals. For example, one sub-goal was to be the top rep. Prospecting is one of those "important" activities that will help achieve it. We intuitively know that. But our days are hectic and it is only when we realize that we are behind in our sales that a sense of urgency is created. It is in Quadrant I that frantically you begin to call. Don't wait for things to become urgent.

What Should You Do?

Start with the classic time management test by listing every single activity you do in a day. Every 15 minutes or so write down everything you have done in that period.

Everything.

Do this all day for at least a week and you will be stunned when you see how you spend your time.

Once you recognize and eliminate your time wasters, you will have more time for important activities like prospecting.

79

Overview of Habits Four, Five, and Six

Habits Four, Five, and Six are habits that are designed to move the sales rep along the continuum of "sales maturity," moving you from a state of independence to a state of interdependence.

Roughly translated, what this means is becoming more "consultative" in your sales approach; a partner with your customer. And while this goal has always been held as an ideal, Habits Four, Five, and Six show you how to achieve it. Here's a brief overview.

Habit Four: Think Win/Win

This is philosophical in nature. It says to be consultative you must always look for solutions that benefit you and your client. Too often, sales reps go for the "quick kill." Yes, they get the sale, but only *that sale*. The customer never buys again.

Thinking win/win also means looking out for your customer and looking out for yourself. Let's face it, there are customers who would love to (and will) take you to the cleaners. That is a lose/win situation. The effective sales professional does not deal in lose/win or win/lose.

Habit 5: Seek First to Understand, Then to Be Understood

It is the habit of communication, and it is something that writers and trainers have been trying to explain for years. Until you fully understand your customer, his needs—personal and business—his company, his customers, his budget . . . you name it . . . you will never be a "partner."Seeking to understand virtually every element of your client's business is key to effective selling. It makes you an integral, perhaps vital, part of your customer's search for solutions.

Habit Six: Synergy

This is the habit of "creative cooperation" between you and the customer to come up with a solution that mutually benefits each of you. It is more than "win/win" and it is significantly more than "just a compromise." It means communicating and working with a "win/win" attitude to produce a solution that is much better, much more sustaining, than a simple compromise. Once you have reached that level, you have truly become "effective" because you are now in a "partnership" mode.

Habits Four, Five, and Six are a more long-term approach to customer relationships. It takes time, patience and strength. It assumes that you, the sales rep, have a solid understanding of the first three habits.

80

Habit Four:
Think Win/Win

D r. Covey entitles the fourth habit: "Think Win/Win." For a sales rep it is not just a cure-all little phrase, but rather a philosophy which should govern your approach to all customer dealings.

In telephone selling, it means that you "win" with the sale, and it means the customer "wins" with the purchase. While this philosophy seems obvious enough, it isn't always the case. Too often, we see two other scenarios which plague the telephone selling world.

Lose/Win

The first scenario is "lose/win." In this situation, the sales rep, (and sometimes the sales manager and the company) are so anxious, so desperate, so fanatical about getting the sale, that they will actually cut prices to the bone or make significant concessions that are virtually impossible to fulfill.

"Lose/win" is short-term thinking. The business world is littered with the casualties of those who "gave away the store" to get the sale. Sooner or later it catches up with you. Thinking or acting lose/win is a slow, painful suicide.

Win/Lose

The second scenario is "win/lose" whereby you win and the customer loses. In this situation, the rep is often pressured to "sell, sell, sell" pump up the value of the sale, exceed quota, lead the pack and line his/her commissioned pockets. It translates into the customer being sold items that perhaps were not necessary or required at the time.

Make absolutely no mistake about it: the customer will

eventually perceive that he/she has been "sold."

The result? Customer enmity and bitterness. Usually you lose the business.

Win/Win is Tough

Covey is quick to remind us that win/win is tough and rigorous. It requires courage and confidence. And he is absolutely right. Sometimes doing what is right for you is not what is right for the customer and vise-versa. It takes courage to stand by your convictions when the customer is making demands on you and your company.

This is not to say that you should not exercise some flexibility in negotiating with the customer. Far from it.

And it is not to say that you should not be cross-selling and up-selling. It is saying, however, that when you think win/win you stop manipulating your customer; there are no hidden agendas. You can be open and more easily understood. It means providing value-added service.

If you have followed and understood the three previous habits, you are equipped to tackle this habit. But, one of the keys to thinking win/win comes from "Habit Five: Seek First to Understand and Then to be Understood." We will tackle that one next.

81

Habit Five: Seek First To Understand, Then To Be Understood

The deepest hunger of customers and prospects is to be understood. They want reps to understand their needs, challenges, strengths, and weaknesses (although they don't always openly demonstrate it).

And it is sometimes tough. But once they are understood, they relax and open up, and the foundation of a solid relationship begins.

Habit Five is not a new concept. "Seek First to Understand, Then to be Understood" is simply another way of saying "learn and listen."

It is the single most important habit that a telesales rep can possess first. Many reps are so bent on delivering their pitch that they fail to "consult" the customer.

Learning to Understand

Know Your Product/Service. There is no mystical, magical potion that will make you a good listener. It's grunt work, plain and simple. Learning to "understand" starts with product/service knowledge. Knowing your product inside and out means having one less thing to worry about (Habit One).

Know Your Objectives. Have clear understanding of what it is you want to achieve as a result of the call. But don't confuse the ultimate goal of "making a sale with objectives." (See Habit

Three). Objectives are the key pieces of information you must obtain before you can even begin to contemplate a sale. Have a prepared list of key questions that must be answered if your goal is to be achieved.

Think "Win/Win" (Habit Four). When you think "win/win" you will slow down and learn. You are not looking for the quick kill on the first call, but rather a good, long-term solution. Take your time and nurture the client. (It will take less time than you think).

Be Prepared. This is a simple suggestion, but all too often ignored. Have everything you need close at hand (product literature, letters, database information, pricing lists, etc.). If you are searching around for material, you won't be listening.

Concentrate Only on the Call. Turn your back to any distractions around you. Avoid overlapping (i.e., don't finish up notes from a previous call, etc.).

When in Doubt, Question. Questioning is an integral part of listening. Sometimes telephone reps fail to ask a question simply because they are too embarrassed to acknowledge that they don't understand.

Take Notes. If there is a trick to listening, it is this. With computer terminals and software programs, the art of using a pad and paper seems to be forgotten. However, I have yet to see a sales rep effectively input "notes" into the terminal while conversing with a customer. Jot down notes during the call, and comprehensive notes after the call. (See pages 90-91 for how to take notes effectively.)

Once you "understand" the customer/prospect, you are positioned for the sixth habit: Synergize (creative problem solving).

82

Habit Six: Synergize

This chapter looks at the efforts of Andrew Z., a telephone sales rep in Montreal who has been the inspiration for this entire set of chapters. Not only does his story help illustrate the sixth habit of highly effective sales reps, but it puts all the other habits into perspective.

The sixth habit is "synergy," or as Dr. Covey calls it, the habit of "creative cooperation." It occurs when two parties use their creative energies to come up with a solution that is better than the solution that each created on their own. Synergy is not compromise. In compromise " 1 + 1 = 1.5." That is a diluted solution that is only somewhat effective.

Synergy, on the other hand, is where " 1 + 1 = 3." The "whole is greater than the sum of its parts."

Andrew's Story

Here is what happened to Andrew. This rep, with over two years experience, works for a reseller of software upgrades offering standard delivery of certain items "within seven working days." (This was due to issues in ordering from the manufacturer, margins and warehousing costs). However, a certain customer required spreadsheet packages within two days for a major project.

The typical compromise solution for the reseller was "rush" service which was offered at a premium. It had always been that way largely because of narrow margins and the amount of time it took to work with the manufacturer. It was never challenged and if a customer did not like it . . . well . . . they learned to accept it or they went elsewhere.

Andrew is a creative problem solver and a superb communicator who had learned a good deal about this customer in previous contacts. Using this information and working with his manager, Andrew proposed a two-day delivery time based on the customer's entire software needs (word processing, graphics and databases) for a six-month period, and not just the spreadsheet packages. What this meant to Andrew's company was a huge sale where the premium could be waived due to the volume, and that the time and energy spent was well worth the effort. What this meant to the customer was a superb delivery time for all its software requirements and a lower price. It was a "synergistic" solution.

Combining all Habits

The sixth habit is more or less the crowning achievement of the other habits. Many sales reps would have given up in the early stages of the sale. Most would have been happy with a compromise: "Let's take a bite on the margin and be glad we got the sale." Clearly, Andrew had a clear vision of what it was he wanted to achieve and took personal responsibility for this project (Habits One and Two). Andrew worked with both his customer and his manager to clearly understand the needs and requirements of both (Habit Five) which obviously resulted in a win/win scenario (Habit Four).

The solution was not a stroke of genius, but rather the putting together of all pieces of the puzzle.

The Seven Habits are not strokes of genius either, but rather a method of helping with that puzzle called "sales."

83

Habit Seven: Sharpening the Saw

Have you ever been too busy driving that you forgot to take time to fill your car with gas? Or have you been so preoccupied that you never quite got around to changing the oil? What can happen? In the first case, your car simply stops running. In the second, it runs poorly for awhile and then finally seizes up. Maintenance is vital for the long-term life of your car. Maintenance is equally vital for the long-term life of your career.

The seventh habit of highly effective sales reps is called "Sharpening the Saw." It is the habit of "self-maintenance." Many sales reps often get so caught up in the process of selling that they don't take the time to "sharpen the saw", i.e., they don't take the time to continuously hone their skills, expand their knowledge, and increase their capacity to be more effective. They believe— wrongly—that selling is the only real maintenance they need.

Four "Saws"

Dr. Covey identifies four "saws" in our lives that need sharpening, and so too with sales reps. He begins by recommending that you take an hour or two each day and devote time to these areas.

Exercise. First, he suggests you spend thirty minutes per day on exercise. On the surface, it would not appear related to sales, but there is a relationship, and it's a good recommendation. Exercise—aerobic exercise—builds up energy, strength and most importantly, stamina. It gives you the physical edge to achieve your goals. Sales isn't easy, and exercise provides a certain amount of "conditioning."

Reading. Not just sales books and literature, but other material that can help expand your knowledge base. Read books on marketing, advertising and finance to help give you a broader understanding of business. Covey also suggests taking the time to think. Think about the process of sales, the process of marketing, and your products, and strategies. Thinking gives perspective; it helps break mindless routine that often serves no purpose. For example, "We have always opened our sales call this way." Think! The question is why? Is there a better way?

Sharpen Your "Mental" Saw. This is important and something you must do to realize your true potential. Sit down daily, even if only for a moment or two, and visualize your goals. See yourself achieving them. Keep your "destination" in sight and in focus at all times. This applies equally to daily goals like the number of sales as it does to longer-term goals like career aspirations.

Focus on "Social and Emotional" Goals. Covey is referring specifically to Habits Four, Five, and Six which generally describe the art of communication and negotiation. While these habits are fundamental to sales success, they also have a spill-over into our personal lives: how we communicate with friends, family and associates.

Just as a vehicle needs fuel and maintenance, so too does a sales rep. Two key points:

> 1. To be an effective sales rep, you must consciously devote time to self-maintenance on a daily basis.

> 2. Self-maintenance means more than reading this book (although it's a good start). It means thinking, visualizing and practicing daily.

What better time to start than now?

84

The Seven Habits Summarized

The Mid-East war with Iraq several years ago provided us with a tremendous reminder of the importance of the integration of strategy with tactics.

Strategy defines the broad strokes of what must be done to achieve an objective while the tactics define how the strategy will be implemented. Strategies tend to focus on the long-term, whereas tactics tend to focus on the short-term. The Allied military forces in the Mid-East had a clearly defined strategy which guided their tactics. The result of the two were obvious.

In essence, the Seven Habits of Highly Effective Sales Reps defines the strategies that are necessary to achieve sales success (however you define it). They identify the longer-term vision of what you must do to meet your goals.

The trouble with the majority of the sales reps I have met and trained is that they do not have a defined strategy. They literally stumble from one call to the next without a clear vision of exactly what they want to achieve. Oh sure, many of them have defined objectives in terms of sales or revenues, but that tends to be short-term. Rarely do I see a rep who is looking one, two or three years down the line. Rarely have I seen one who has a "philosophy" about their approach to sales. The Seven Habits build that philosophy.

Strategies and tactics work hand in hand— but most reps do not understand this relationship. The average salesperson focuses and works on techniques (tactics). And in many cases, the results are very good. But, if you can orchestrate the techniques with an overall strategy, the results will not be good— they will be phenomenal!

Go to Work!

Here's how to start: Grab a sheet of paper. Now. At the top of the sheet draw a circle, and inside it write specific goals or a set of goals. List the Seven Habits down the side leaving space between each habit for notes. (The habits define your strategy for achieving your goals.)

Review the chapters on the Seven Habits so that you have a clear understanding of what each means.

In the reserved space between each habit list the tactics (sometimes called "action items") you will need to execute to implement the strategy. You might realize you are doing many of the action items already. Great! But you should also find that there are action items that require implementation. Concentrate on these items.

Finally, review the plan twice per day: once in the morning and once in the afternoon.

Congratulations! You now have a clearly defined plan which integrates your strategies with your tactics. But don't be fooled. This is just a beginning. You will find that your action items will change and vary constantly, but your strategies (habits) should remain constant. Good luck!

Conclusion

Well, you have made it to the end of the book. Good stuff!

You have managed to do what the majority of sales reps simply do not. You have *invested* in your career and in your self-development. You are one of the few. And chances are, you are one of the few that will do exceptionally well. Congratulations!

As you read the book you might not have realized many startling revelations. Much of the material you either knew or perhaps intuitively understood—and that's good. I had two objectives in mind when writing the book. The first was to bring you perspective. By offering proven ideas, tips and techniques from across North America I presented the collective experience of hundreds of telephone and field representatives. Hopefully, their wisdom gave you a new "look" or provided a twist on a variety of situations and circumstances in the selling process.

The second objective was to help you improve your selling and lead generation activities by one or two percent in a dozen, two dozen or even a hundred different areas. The idea was that the combined improvement in all these ideas would have a significant effect on your bottom line results.

The next challenge you face is to actually implement some of these ideas. It will be hard at first. Anything new . . . any change introduced into your routine is tough. Don't expect overnight results. Rarely does that happen (but sometimes it does!) Stick to it. Have the discipline. As I am sure you are aware a habit (good or bad) takes about three weeks to become internalized and part of your subconscious. So have patience, fellow teleprofessional.

The journey of sales never, ever ends. So never let yourself coast, regardless of how well things seem to be going. There is only one way to coast: downhill.

This is just the beginning. Reading this book is a great start. As I said, you already have an edge on most of your competitors (and your fellow workers). Don't stop the process of learning. Continue it. Invest in more books. Purchase newsletters. Buy tapes and videos. Attend seminars. (See information to follow from "Business By Phone" which is the best place to start!) Share your ideas. Create an article or two or your own and submit them to your industry trade publication, or to the *Telephone Selling Report* newsletter. Join a learning group. Find and develop a mentor. Leverage your supervisor or manager.

And finally, call me or write me to share your ideas, anxieties, frustrations and joys. I want to hear from you. Let's start a dialogue.

Keep the momentum going!

Jim Domanski

Teleconcepts Consulting

613 591 1998 - telephone

613 591 1707 - fax

jdomanski@igs.net

35 Vanstone Drive

Kanata, Ontario Canada, K2L 1W4

Here Are Other Resources You Can Get Right Now to Help You Manage, Motivate, and SELL!

Go to Our Website for Lots of FREE Telesales Tips, Special Offers, and Other Resources to Help You

www.BusinessByPhone.com

FREE! "The TelE-Sales Hot Tips of the Week" Newsletter

Each week you will have sales tips and words of motivation from Art Sobczak e-mailed to your desk, free! Sign up by e-mailing to **arts @businessbyphone.com** with "join" in the subject line, or go to **www.businessbyphone.com** and sign up yourself. Plus, you will get a free special report for simply sigining up.

The Telesales Rep College Two-Day Training Workshops

Throughout the year we deliver 8-10 public training programs across the U.S., covering every step of the professional telesales call. Valuable for rookies and veterans alike, you'll leave energized, armed with new ideas to deploy right away to grab more business on your very next call. Only 30 participants accepted per session.Call 1-800-326-7721 for the current schedule.

To Get More Copies of This Book:

To get additional copies of this book, photocopy or remove this form, or call or fax us with the necessary information. *(Inquire about quantity discounts. Also, bookstore and dealer inquiries welcome.)*

Yes, please send me _____ copies of *"Profiting By Phone"* at $29.00 (U.S. funds) each (+$3.50 shipping in the U.S., $7 Canada, overseas charged at cost.)

Name_____

Company_____

Address_____

City_____State_____Zip Code_____

Phone_____

Fax_____

Method of Payment

❑ Visa/MC/AMEX/Discover

#_____

sig._____exp._____

❑ Check /Money Order Enclosed *(U.S. Funds Only)*

Ways to Order

• **Phone** your order to **1-800-326-7721**, or (402)895-9399.

• **Fax** your order to (402)896-3353.

• **Mail** your order to Business By Phone, 13254-B1 Stevens St., Omaha, NE, 68137.

• **E-Mail** your order to arts@businessbyphone.com.